'Thomson spins a complex tale of pilgrims, politics and mountaineering mythology from his diverse sources ... *Nanda Devi* is ... a spirited homage to a remote, awesome landscape. Rich in detail and light of tone, it teases its stories out slowly and gently and, by playing down the physical discomforts, will make non-climbers want to travel to the Sanctuary' Chris Moss, *Daily Telegraph*

'A tantalising glimpse of this fragile, harshly beautiful place' *Global*

'Thomson has a nose for stories ... [And] the photographs picture the sensational and, yes, holy landscape in which all the events he describes took place' *Guardian*

'The book offers a ... welcome escape to somewhere rare and wonderful' Anthony Sattin, *Sunday Times*

'Thomson tells a story that has to do with politics, ecology and history, as much as with the strenuous adventure in a beautiful setting that his book so vividly celebrates'
Independent

'Eloquently lays out the often bizarre, and always interesting history of this remote area and its explorers, as well as charting the author's own expedition into the sanctuary ... Informative, yet never dry, the book offers an insight into a place of near mythical status and takes the reader where they will never have the chance to go'
...venture Travel

The White Rock

'*The White Rock* is the long-awaited definitive travel book on Peru' John Hemming

'A riveting account of South American exploration and Peruvian culture, full of unforgettable stories and amazing facts' *Bookseller*

'A record of one man's obsession with the Incas over a period of 20 years: an obsession that led him to search out (and in one case discover) Inca ruins in the most inaccessible places, far beyond the reach of tourists'
Anthony Daniels, *Sunday Telegraph*

'It is a measure of Hugh Thomson's skill as a writer, historian and explorer that *The White Rock* is such a pleasure' Justin Marozzi, *The Spectator*

'Time and time again he brings the Incas to life as real people' Matthew Parris, 'A Good Read', *Radio 4*

'Hugh Thomson has played off the Indiana Jones heroics and Klaus Kinski jungle madness of the genre against respectable archaeology and anthropology ... This is Bruce Chatwin with *cojones*. More than that, it is a micro-allegory of the saga of fantasy, bravado, conquest, and frustration that is the collective narrative of the Inca hunters' Andy Martin, *Independent*

'It is Thomson's generosity of spirit which stands out and makes this a great book. He presents a faithful description of Inca history and of life in modern-day Peru, while preserving fascinating pen portraits of those figures involved in the decline of the Incas and in the revival of interest in their lost world. It is a work that is both accessible and academically rigorous'

Isabel Cockayne, *Eastern Daily Express*

Hugh Thomson read English at Cambridge University. He has led several expeditions to the Peruvian Andes, which he describes in *The White Rock: An Exploration of the Inca Heartland*. As a film-maker he has won many awards for his documentaries, which include *Indian Journeys* and *Dancing in the Street: A Rock and Roll History*. More details can be found at www.thewhiterock.co.uk.

'Everywhere Thomson goes, he finds good stories to tell' *New York Times Review of Books*

By Hugh Thomson

Nanda Devi: A Journey to the Last Sanctuary
The White Rock: An Exploration of the Inca Heartland
Lost City of the Incas (*as editor, also critical Introduction and illustrations*)
Machu Picchu and the Camera

NANDA DEVI

A JOURNEY TO THE LAST SANCTUARY

....

HUGH THOMSON

PHOENIX

A PHOENIX PAPERBACK

First published in Great Britain in 2004
by Weidenfeld & Nicolson
This paperback edition published in 2005
by Phoenix,
an imprint of Orion Books Ltd,
Orion House, 5 Upper St Martin's Lane,
London WC2H 9EA

A CIP catalogue record for this book
is available from the British Library.

ISBN 0 75381 847 7

Typeset by Butler and Tanner Ltd, Frome and London
Printed and bound in Great Britain by
Clays Ltd, St Ives plc

www.orionbooks.co.uk

CONTENTS

ILLUSTRATIONS

Line drawings by Bip Pares, originally used in Eric
   Shipton, *Nanda Devi* (1936).

Section One
The Alaknanda Ganges leading to the High Himalaya.
Hindu pilgrims celebrating *aarti* near Rishikesh.
Rainbow over the Dhaoli Ganges.
Steve Berry.
Landscape above Lata.
The untouched forests of the Nanda Devi Sanctuary.
Dewan Singh Butola, a porter on the Shipton and Tilman
   expeditions in the 1930s.
Inside the Nanda Devi Sanctuary at twilight.
Mount Changabang, 'the shining mountain'.
Cairns marking the entrance to the Sanctuary.
Mount Nanda Devi, partially hidden.
George Band, with the outer 'curtain wall' of the
   Sanctuary behind him.
John Shipton collecting seeds on the slopes above Lata.
Mount Trisul.
Colonel Narinder 'Bull' Kumar.
Nanda Devi at the head of the Rishi Ganges gorge.

All photographs © Hugh Thomson 2003 unless otherwise stated.

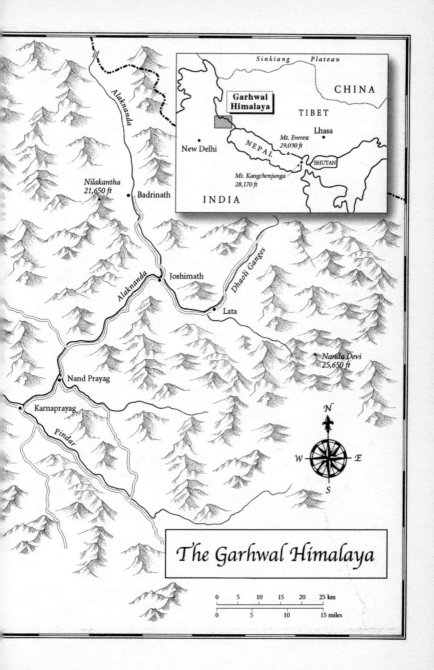

The Garhwal Himalaya

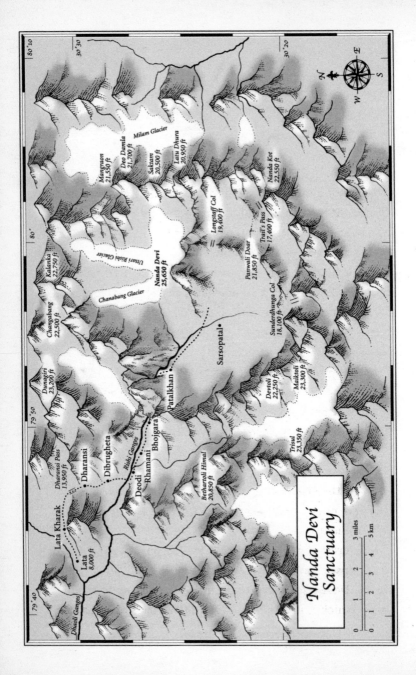

Nanda Devi Sanctuary

Milam Glacier

Mangraon
21,550 ft

Deo Damla
21,700 ft

Saltam
20,500 ft

Latu Dhura
20,950 ft

Nanda Kot
22,550 ft

Longstaff Col
19,600 ft

Kalanka
22,750 ft

Uttari Rishi Glacier

Nanda Devi
25,650 ft

Chanabang Glacier

Pamvali Doar
21,850 ft

Trail's Pass
17,400 ft

Changabang
22,500 ft

Sunderdhunga Col
18,100 ft

Dunagiri
23,200 ft

Sarsopatal

Devtoli
22,250 ft

Maiktoli
23,300 ft

Patalkhan

Rishi Ganges

Bhojgara

Dharansi Pass
13,950 ft

Dharansi

Dibrugheta

Deodi

Rhamani

Trisul
23,350 ft

Bethartoli Himal
20,850 ft

Lata Kharak

Lata
8,000 ft

Dhauli Ganges

N
E
W
S

3 miles
5 km

0 1 2 3
0 1 2 3 4 5

INTRODUCTION

This is not a book about climbing, nor do I claim to be a climber. It is a book about mountains – and one mountain in particular, Nanda Devi, which lies in the Himalaya, on the border between India and Tibet.

More than perhaps any other of the great Himalayan peaks (as Everest only became famous comparatively late, for reasons of geographical suprematism), a powerful blend of myth and politics has always swirled around Nanda Devi. A rare opportunity to travel there gave me the chance to explore that myth.

Following the recent books marking the fiftieth anniversary of the 1953 ascent of Everest, this is also a chance to hark back to an earlier and gentler mountaineering world, that of Eric Shipton and H.W. 'Bill' Tilman in the pre-war period. Shipton and Tilman roamed happily through the Garhwal in a spirit of innocent adventuring that has now been lost; Nanda Devi was their greatest achievement.

If Everest is a mountain that has become littered with the corpses and detritus of previous expeditions, then Nanda Devi remains the epitome of the inviolate mountain – which is perhaps what mountains should be about.

ACKNOWLEDGEMENTS

In writing about Nanda Devi I am very conscious that I am adding another stone to the cairn left by writers of previous generations who travelled there: Eric Shipton, H.W. Tilman, Charles Houston, J.-J. Languepin, W.H. Murray and many more, to all of whom I owe a debt.

My thanks also to William Dalrymple, who introduced me to the Garhwal, and to Bill Aitken for his first enticing descriptions of Nanda Devi.

In India, I was given assistance by Yatish Bahaguna, Harish Chandola, S. Gautham, Harish Kapadia and Jane Sabherwal, while my travelling companions on previous journeys in the southern Himalaya included Simon Ffrench, Nandu Kumar, Joanna Lumley, Laura Marshall, Toby Strong and Chris Vile.

Members of the Nanda Devi 2000 Expedition who have given advice and occasional prompts include George Band, Albert Chapman, Ian and Loreto McNaught-Davis, and John Shipton.

I am particularly indebted to Jeff Ford for his hospitality and bibliographical knowledge, and to Steve Berry for his continued help and for getting us there in the first place.

I would also like to thank the other members of the expedition: David Baber, Gerald Becker, Barry Bond, Natalena Dacunha, Sorab Darius N. Gandhi, Howard Humphreys, Colonel Narinder 'Bull' Kumar, Akshay Kumar, Bimal Kumar, David Sayer and Alan Tate, as well as the many porters and support staff without whom it would not have been possible. On a large expedition, to give a detailed account of every member's activities throughout would require the plot and length of a Russian novel. I have therefore restricted myself to tell the stories of those I had most contact with; this is not meant to diminish in any way the contributions of those others whom I have not 'tracked' so assiduously.

Bishen Singh helped me take photographs of the Sanctuary. Audrey Salkeld gave advice on the archive images used. The maps, as with *The White Rock*, have been ably rendered by John Gilkes.

Those who read the manuscript include Steve Berry, Arabella Cecil, Jeff Ford, S. Gautham, Fiona Heren, Richard Taylor, Sara Taylor and various patient members of my family. Dr Julius J. Lipner advised me on a point of Hindu theology.

I am also grateful to Francine Brody and Richard Milner at Weidenfeld & Nicolson, and my agent Georgina Capel.

It is hard to conceive of a bowl, full of luxuriant grass and flowers of delicate hue; of partridges calling to each other across the gay scene; of *bharals* contentedly ruminating from their high, rocky, silent perches; of all this warm and secluded life enclosed by an icy, impassable and treacherous ring of high mountains, where blizzards blow constantly and living things do not dare to venture. But such is the reality of the Nanda Devi Sanctuary.

Narinder 'Bull' Kumar
'Nanda Devi: Indian Mountaineering Expedition 1964'

So on he fares, and to the border comes
Of EDEN, where delicious Paradise,
Now nearer, Crowns with her enclosure green,
As with a rural mound the champain head
Of a steep wilderness, whose hairie sides
With thicket overgrown, grottesque and wilde,
Access deni'd; and over head up grew
Insuperable highth of loftiest shade,
Cedar, and Pine, and Firr, and branching Palm,
A Silvan Scene, and as the ranks ascend
Shade above shade, a woodie Theatre
Of stateliest view. Yet higher then thir tops
The verdurous wall of Paradise up sprung.

John Milton, *Paradise Lost*

If mountains were just lumps of rock there would be no point in climbing them, but they are the repository of dreams.

Imagine one of the tallest mountains in the world. A high and beautiful valley curls around it like a moat, filled with the rarest of flowers and animals.

Now imagine also that around this valley is a ring of Himalayan tooth-edged peaks, linked to each other by an impenetrable curtain wall of sheer cliffs, which form a protective guard for the mountain at their centre. Then circle this protective wall with another 'moat' and another high wall of peaks, so that there is both an inner and outer keep, like the fortifications of a medieval castle. Allow just one entrance to the valley sanctuary at the heart of this complex – a river gorge that drains the mountains' glaciers, and cuts through the inner and outer curtain walls in a chasm of such breathtaking steepness and ferocity that even the most hardened of travellers turns away from it in despair.

In some ways it is easy to imagine such a place – because literature has already pictured it, many times. The idea of the 'sanctuary', the earthly paradise, is as old as Eden and is common to both Western and Eastern religions. More recently, Hollywood has perpetuated it as a recurring archetype, the 'Lost World' or 'Shangri-La', which explorers try to reach at their peril.

But such a place exists in reality. It is called the Nanda Devi Sanctuary, in the Himalaya between India and Tibet. And the torrent that issues from its formidable gates is one of the sources of the Ganges, perhaps the world's most revered river.

The often tragic history of those who have tried to reach it shows what happens when the dream of finding a sanctuary, one of mankind's oldest and most compulsive quests, collides with solid rock. In the past, Nanda Devi has claimed many lives.

For many years it has been closed to all outsiders because of its position on the border with Tibet; such complete inaccessibility has only increased its appeal. This is the story of how, for a brief moment, the gates to the Sanctuary were opened.

*

'Hugh, we think we may have managed to secure permission from the Indian Government to take a small expedition to the Nanda Devi Sanctuary. Do you want to come?'

Steve Berry spoke with his customary care and deliberation, like a county solicitor explaining a land sale, but he didn't need to tell me how excited he was; we both knew exactly why Nanda Devi had attained a near-mythical appeal to climbers and travellers.

I had heard of the Sanctuary and how difficult it was to enter when I had travelled previously in the Indian Himalaya. Like all that is both beautiful and forbidden, it had immediately tempted me.

It took all of three seconds to make up my mind.

'Of course I'll come.'

'I knew you would,' said Steve.

*

I was lying on my back in the swimming pool of the Oberoi Maidens Hotel in Delhi, floating. Each time I started to drift into a daydream, a flock of green parakeets would fly directly overhead with a clatter that was amplified underwater. Higher up were the kites, idly wheeling, perhaps attracted by the spectacle of a motionless white Englishman on the surface of the water. It was September, a good time of year in Delhi, the turning point from monsoon lassitude to autumnal sun. I was re-birthing in India.

This is where I had begun and ended every Indian journey. It was midday and strictly speaking too hot to be in a pool ('Just for the honey-mooners,' as the old Delhi diplomatic and journalistic hands say), but I had a well-organised routine. Ten minutes floating, then I'd heave myself out to a waiting lime soda, before repeating the cycle back in the water. I wanted that weightlessness that you can only achieve when jet-lagged and disorientated. After a dawn arrival, I was already well on my way, having had just a few hours of disturbed sleep in a room redolent of the Indian mustiness of linen still drying somewhere.

The rest of the expedition were likewise awakening slowly from their cocoons all around the hotel. But I had no desire to meet or talk to anyone else yet. I needed to come round slowly. And given what life would be like once we got to northern India and the Garhwal, I wanted every last moment of luxury I could squeeze from the tube.

The pool had the familiar, slow rhythms that I enjoyed: the attendant issuing me with towels, drinks on a silver salver and a drip-feed of cheese pakoras on a linen-spread tray. On previous visits to Delhi, usually staying in cheap guesthouses, I had walked into the grandest of hotels – the Imperial, the Taj – and signed myself into the pool as a fictitious guest. Nothing felt better than that first illicit length.

These big hotels were central to Delhi life in a way I had never experienced in any other city. Local residents would come from their security-controlled compounds in the Lodhi Gardens or Golf Links to patrol the hotel malls and power-lunch in the restaurants. Meetings were always in the 'Coffee Shop' of a hotel. It could come as a surprise to remember that they had foreign tourists staying there as well.

The Oberoi Maidens was not in this category. It was smaller and on the wrong side of town, in the Old City near the Red Fort and Jama Masjid. As I drove away from it in a battered Ambassador, it was good to have the sounds of old Delhi blow through the car, punctuated by the passing scooter bells that seemed to hang suspended in the noonday heat before fading away. It was for this reason that I liked the yellow taxis of the street, even if they were more unreliable than the hotels' air-conditioned ones. On one memorable occasion the steering wheel of an Ambassador had come off in the driver's hands as we drove and we had glided to a graceful halt in the gutter of one of Lutyens' finest boulevards.

I was going to see Bill Aitken, the one man in Delhi I never met in a hotel but always in his own home. I'd first come across Bill when I was travelling the Hindu pilgrimage route through the Himalaya and had immediately taken to his intriguing mixture of Indian inclusiveness and Calvinist rigour. He also knew the hills like the back of his hand.

I had already rung him before leaving England for advice about the Nanda Devi expedition, as he was one of the few people I knew who had been there. He had given me no practical guidance at all, but had simply said: 'In climbing to the Sanctuary, it helps to have a belief in something, anything, that endures.'

Now he was waiting for me at the door of his house, intense blue eyes peering out beneath a Himachal Pradesh hat perched jauntily on cropped silver hair.

Bill was a maverick. He described himself as 'Scottish by birth, naturalised Indian by choice'. He had hitchhiked to India in 1959 to live in an ashram, which proved only a partial success, in that while deeply drawn to Hinduism he had equally resisted its institutionalisation. After some years, he had in his words 'escaped' the ashram, together with Prithvi, his future wife, whom he'd met there. Together they'd spent forty years happily wandering the subcontinent, often by train – he had a fetish for steam engines – sometimes by foot, as with the pilgrimages, and increasingly, I now learnt, by motorbike.

After so many years, the cadence of Bill's thought and speech had become Anglo-Indian: 'Actually, I only got my motorbike comparatively recently. And I bought it off a chap at the garage down here and climbed aboard, never having ridden it, and actually came up just outside the Savoy Hotel in Mussoorie and rode straight into an Ambassador. The driver charged me five hundred rupees' compensation. As in life, they say, get your disasters over early. So I was quite happy to have a disaster, titanic, on day one.

'The motorbike is a marvellous way to travel. But I mean, you have to know how to take hill bends. It's like chewing hill food – chew lightly, swallow hard. Go in wide and come out on the hill side.'

As we had done so many times before, Bill and I sat in his garden, drinking tea under the jacaranda as we circled around the subject in hand. Occasionally Prithvi would come out and remind Bill that he should be working, or paying her more attention, but Bill would dismiss this with an airy wave of the hand and continue talking about Nanda Devi.

It had first become famous in the early nineteenth century when the sahibs and their memsahibs had retreated up into the Indian foothills of the Himalaya, to places like Mussoorie and Ranikhet. Soon the more intrepid of the early British travellers had penetrated beyond these hill stations to the formidable High Himalaya, where mountains such as Kamet, Trisul, Changabang and Dunagiri lined the horizon. And the greatest of all these was Mount Nanda Devi, whose name means 'the bliss-giving goddess'.

'Of course,' said Bill, 'the amusing thing about the Empire attitude was the idea that we started the idea of hill stations where we could aestivate' (he stopped to enjoy the word) 'and cut the summer heat, but in actual fact it was the Hindu gods who started this notion of wintering in the lower regions and spending the summer in the snowy heights. Long before the Alpine Club was founded, the Hindu gods – and goddesses – had cottoned on to the idea that the mountains were a wonderful place to be in the hot weather.' Bill beamed with pleasure at the thought.

A few of these early adventurers managed to climb the high peaks that made up the 'inner wall' around Nanda Devi, but could only look down with longing at the Sanctuary below; the cliff walls fell away with such ferocity that, even today, no one has ever descended them.

For the British, Nanda Devi quickly became one of the great mountaineering goals and for one simple reason: at 25,640 feet, it was not only the highest mountain in India, but the highest mountain in the whole British Empire. Yet no one could even get to its base, let alone climb it. For almost a century the Alpine Club puzzled over the conundrum of how to enter the elusive Sanctuary. The best of three generations of climbers all made the attempt and failed.

At least Everest allowed a frontal assault on its terrors; Mallory died there with Irvine in 1924. But by 1934, a decade later, the British had still not found a way into the Sanctuary, let alone set foot on Nanda Devi itself.

It had not been for want of trying. Every possible approach route had been tried. In 1883 the colourful Scottish mountaineer W.W. Graham (one of the first to come to the Himalaya simply to enjoy himself, rather than for any spurious scientific reason) had attempted to enter the Sanctuary from the west, but had turned back, appalled, when he saw the Rishi Ganges gorge. Then in 1905, Tom Longstaff, the leading climber of his day, had unsuccessfully explored the eastern approaches; he returned two years later to try equally unsuccessfully to penetrate it from the north.

The next wave of attempts came after the First World War. In 1926 Hugh Ruttledge, together with the Everest veteran Howard Somervell, endeavoured to get in from the north-east. They failed. Ruttledge tried twice more, in 1927 and 1932, before writing to *The Times* in frustration: 'Nanda Devi imposes upon her votaries an admission test as yet beyond their skill and endurance.'

The Sanctuary had been probed from every angle. As Bill reminded me, there had been no less than eight attempts to reach it. Each expedition had demanded a long trek in over the foothills and a complicated circumnavigation of the enormous Nanda Devi massif; Ruttledge described this as 'a seventy-mile barrier ring, on which stand twelve measured peaks over 21,000 [feet] high ... the Rishi Ganges gorge, rising at the foot of Nanda Devi, and draining an area of some two hundred and fifty square miles of snow and ice, has carved for itself what must be one of the most terrific gorges in the world'. The Sanctuary, said Ruttledge, 'was more inaccessible than the North Pole'.

It was left to two outsiders, Eric Shipton and H.W. 'Bill' Tilman, to pull off one of the most romantic and audacious of mountaineering coups. They had known each other as coffee planters in Kenya. Shipton had joined the odd expedition before, but no one had ever heard of Tilman. When they went to Nanda Devi in 1934, Shipton was just twenty-six, Tilman some ten years older.

Going completely against the custom of the time, they avoided the usual large military-style expeditions, with endless porters and a string of base camps, considered to be the only way to 'conquer' such peaks. Instead the two set off alone, with just a shirt each, intending, as they put it, 'to live off the land'. They relied on the skills and instincts of a few hand-picked Sherpas, and shared all they had with them, much to the horror of those senior members of the Alpine Club for whom Sherpas, like servants, should be kept at a suitable distance.

Over two successive and punishing seasons, Shipton and Tilman managed somehow to find a way along the precipitous Ganges gorge and into the Sanctuary, so becoming the first human beings to set foot on the base of Mount Nanda Devi. Two years later Tilman returned and climbed to the summit. Ruttledge acclaimed their achievement as 'one of the greatest feats in mountaineering history'. It was the highest peak that had ever been climbed.

Then came the Second World War and an end to exploration in the area. The mountain remained largely undisturbed until the 1970s. Its close proximity to the border with Chinese-occupied Tibet made it militarily sensitive to newly independent India. Those fears were realised in 1962 with the Indo-China War, when the success of the Chinese incursion against Nehru's government only heightened security issues. An 'Inner-Line' was drawn across the map almost parallel to India's international border, so as to create a safety buffer-zone beyond which foreigners or Indians were not supposed to travel without special permission.

After 1974, the 'Inner-Line' restriction was lifted and some expeditions were allowed access to Nanda Devi, but by 1982 the government had decided that the Sanctuary should be completely closed, claiming that expeditions might destroy the fragility of what had previously been a self-contained ecosystem.

So for twenty years it had been an inaccessible place, a legend whose appeal had grown precisely because, in a world where seemingly everywhere is open to the traveller, Nanda Devi was closed. Until now.

'And how,' asked Bill, with a quick and astute glance over his teacup, 'have you managed to get in?'

'Because the expedition is being led by John Shipton and "Bull" Kumar.'

John Shipton was Eric Shipton's son. And Colonel Narinder 'Bull' Kumar was probably India's most famous living mountaineer. He had led the first Indian team to climb Nanda Devi in 1964, only the second successful attempt after Tilman's. It had needed a dream ticket pairing like that to persuade a reluctant Indian Government to let us in. But just as extra insurance, Steve Berry, who had coordinated the whole expedition, had brought in Ian McNaught-Davis, a friend of Chris Bonington's and the President of the International Mountaineering and Climbing Federation, so a political heavyweight in every way. Even then, Steve Berry had told me, it had taken years of persuasion to get permission, and we were going only to the Nanda Devi Sanctuary, not to climb the mountain itself.

'But do you know why they were so reluctant to let anybody in?' said Bill, his eyes laughing. I gave the official reason: that the Sanctuary needed to be left undisturbed for ecological reasons.

'Since when did the Indian Government ever do anything for ecological reasons? I think you'll find it was a little more than that. But I'll leave you to work it out for yourself when you go.

'And good luck.'

*

I saw Colonel Narinder 'Bull' Kumar for the first time when I arrived back at the hotel. A tough compact-looking man, now in his seventies, he was getting into a taxi with John Shipton to collect a last necessary bit of paperwork from the Indian authorities.

He had been nicknamed 'Bull' by his army boxing coach when he first joined the army and I still wouldn't have fancied facing him in a ring. He had a resilient physique and the greying remains of a moustache that I knew from photos had once been one of India's finest.

Steve Berry was just inside the hotel lobby, having seen them off. He was understandably nervous that there should be no last-minute bureaucratic delays after all his hard work in getting us here.

Steve was an intriguing mix. When describing a potential trip, he always spoke with the care and deliberation of someone suggesting a possible legal course of action — possibly because it was to some extent a legal course of action. He was conscious of his status as head of Himalayan Kingdoms, the operating company for the expedition, which at the end of the day would be liable if anything went wrong.

He was also meticulous. Steve had helped me plan various film-shoots. By the time we'd finished each one, we would have been through a dozen schedules as he plotted each small change and variant into the scheme. I could still remember his air of infinite patience and resignation as he'd said: 'So, Hugh, what you're really saying is that you want to stop for lunch after just three hours' trekking, not four?'

I had got to know him as we planned those films together; he was one of those people whose quiet strengths grow on you. Steve had long been part of the Bristol climbing scene in the UK, but had also been frequently drawn back to the Himalaya for many of his fifty-odd years, perhaps because he had been born in India and had imbibed his father's climbing stories about Kashmir from an early age.

In some ways Steve reminded me of a veteran rocker, a member of one of the sixties bands he so admired, like Quiksilver Messenger Service; someone who had been on the road a long time, had learnt the business the hard way, but who still kept a bit of rebellious rock and roll flickering away underneath it all.

He had financed this expedition through Himalayan Kingdoms by assembling a group of 'big-name' mountaineers, and then selling the rest of the places on the team. This was common practice, although it could run the risk of creating a very mixed-ability group. And I was the joker in the pack, the writer who had been asked to join, with a background more in exploration than as a mountaineer.

To be honest, I was a little nervous about meeting some of the other expedition members who were waiting inside. Steve had assembled a glittering star cast and I wasn't sure I lived up to the headline acts at the top of the billing. As well as John Shipton, 'Bull' Kumar and Ian McNaught-Davis, all names to conjure with, there was George Band, who had been a member of the successful 1953 British expedition to Everest.

I'd never met him before, but he was instantly recognisable as he ambled around the group. Although the Everest expedition had been half a century ago, George was still a large man, exuding reassurance, geniality and experience. In the decades since, he had climbed on every continent. Tall and white-haired, he had the loping, slightly bow-legged gait of a man who has been rolling down from summits all his life.

Indeed, the whole group looked much older than I had imagined. At forty, I was the youngest. In the main, these were mountain men who had grown up on the legend of Nanda Devi and had now come to see it in the flesh. When I'd made the mistake of telling my wife that George Band was making the trip, aged seventy-one, she had immediately assumed that the whole thing would be a picnic. In fact, after a lifetime of climbing, George was by some length one of the fittest of us all. Stamina often increases in the mountains with age. There are few young men of twenty who don't have better mountain legs by the time they're older, if they haven't fallen off the rope (or the wagon) in the meantime.

I noticed that George was writing down everyone's name in a pocketbook, so as to learn them. This might have seemed pedantic, but was born of long experience of the way that such expeditions work, or don't. A group of people who hardly know each other, sometimes of different nationalities, are brought together to attempt a difficult mission. Often at great speed they arrive at base camp and shortly afterwards will be in a position where they may need to rely on each other totally for survival. The process of 'getting to know your companions' can never begin too early and is frequently left too late.

'You're Peru, aren't you?' said George. I knew what he meant. It was where most of my expeditions had been. It turned out that George had once led an expedition to climb Mount Pumasillo in the Peruvian Andes, near my old hunting ground close to Machu Picchu. As George now freely admitted, they had failed to climb Pumasillo. Indeed, they had not even managed to find it, returning chastened and 'with a little more respect for Peruvian gorges'. If this was intended to put me at my ease, it worked. In fact, George was so wholly at ease with himself that he relaxed everyone around him.

It was a genial group standing around the bar. There were seventeen of us and I knew myself too well to hope that I would begin to emulate George and take them all in. As far as I was concerned, it was hard enough to learn one name in a day, let alone seventeen. But I was sure that the faces would slowly coalesce into characters.

*

One face very forcibly turned into a character over the next few days, as we began the approach route up north from Delhi and into the Himalaya.

Ian McNaught-Davis was universally known as Mac. He may have been President of the International Mountaineering and Climbing Federation, but Mac was not your soft-shoe-shuffle sort of politician. He also swore more than anyone I'd ever met. A blunt Yorkshireman who'd been climbing all his life, he called a spade 'a fucking spade'.

I was not sure that the tranquil Indian Garhwal was quite ready for him. A large, naturally florid man, his face had got even redder as we advanced across the Indian plain; he brought a touch of *Viz* to the Himalaya.

His reaction on being told that we were now entering the temperance holy towns alongside the Ganges was not good: 'Don't they know it's part of *our* fucking religion to have beer every day? Don't they understand that? I mean, what would happen if we all went and bathed in the fucking Thames every day? It's fucking ridiculous!'

He was calmed by his Chilean wife Loreto, also a member of the expedition. Loreto was one of the two women with us, the other being Natalena Dacunha, a cosmopolitan computer specialist from Holland. The theory was that having women on a team made for a calmer, less macho atmosphere. If so, no one had ever explained this to Mac.

The constant flow of expletives rolled over all comers, regardless of sex, religion or, for that matter, whether they understood a word he was saying. Perhaps luckily, his strong Yorkshire accent was often incomprehensible to any puzzled Garhwalis who overheard him.

Yet even though he could come on like Oliver Reed the morning after, Mac had immense charm as well and one sterling merit: you always knew precisely what he was thinking, because he always told you.

Given his earlier outburst, Mac took it calmly when I suggested later that we stop and do a bit of bathing in the Ganges ourselves. We were just beyond Rishikesh, where the Ganges roars down out of the Himalaya in a series of torrents that have made it popular with white-water rafting groups. I knew of a guesthouse with a bathing pool. After eight hours of journeying from Delhi in a bus, it was too good to pass by.

The Glass House was an old maharajah's lodge from pre-Independence days, when it had been common practice for the Indian aristocracy to build such lodges by the Ganges so that they could hold their river *puja* ceremonies in privacy – a practice still continued by the rich today. Next door to the Glass House, I noticed a mansion owned by the millionaire Thapar family, with a helicopter pad so that they could make their *puja* and be back in Delhi in time for dinner at the Imperial or the Sheraton.

The Rajasthani staff greeted me with all the pleasure of seeing the return of a high-rolling customer (I'd made a film there and had taken over the guesthouse for some weeks). They still had that air of slight sadness that I remembered, exiles from Rajasthan living at an uncomfortably higher altitude, with cold winters and an impoverished diet. One of them had told me with some disgust, 'All these bloody mountain people eat is dhal,' and, although they were more polite than Mac in saying so, the lack of alcohol didn't help either.

My companions looked dubious as I stripped off and went into the water, which was slate-grey and fast flowing. I felt dubious myself when I remembered that while the Ganges might look idyllic here in the almost deserted gorge – a few sandbanks, the gardens of the Glass House coming down to the river's edge, the call of a sand plover – upstream there lived most of the considerable population of the Garhwal. Still, it felt good and there were quite a few sins I could do with washing away. When the others saw I wasn't going to get swept down to Rishikesh, a few came in after me, including John Shipton.

I hadn't talked much to John before. He looked like his father – deceptively slight, but wiry and tough – and spoke in the same quiet and slightly mumbling way that people remembered of Eric. But there was an intensity about him that attracted me from our very first conversation. Almost his first words were: 'I'm trying to exorcise some bloody ghosts here,' with a wave of his hand at the expedition convoy, and then he fell silent, letting the words hang between us. I soon learnt that conversation with John had its own rhythm, with abrupt fits and starts.

We were the only ones having a cup of chai and a paratha from the roadside stall near the bathing pool, as most of the others were giving Indian food a wide berth. Like me, John had previously walked the *yatra* pilgrimage trails in the hills above us.

When he started again, we talked of other parts of the world that we had both trekked in – the Sierra Madre Oriental in Mexico, the Western High Atlas in Morocco – and then circled back to the current expedition.

'I've always kept away from this stuff because of all the organisation that goes with it' (he waved again at the others). 'Not my thing at all.' John was a loner and so very much in his father's mould. The distinguishing feature of Eric Shipton's mountaineering career had been his mistrust of big teams.

'I always remember the old man telling me a story about his Nanda Devi trip – that when he was coming back with Tilman, and they were heading off towards Kedarnath, they looked down from a pass on this beautiful valley full of bamboos, and from up high it had looked easy to cross, a day's work at most – but it took them weeks and weeks and weeks. Things always look different from far away.'

John fell silent. Then he spoke again, this time about the *yatra* trail that his father and Tilman had taken between Kedarnath and Gangotri. This was one of the traditional high pilgrimage routes that the Indian holy men, the *sadhus*, follow between the great shrines at the head of the four tributaries of the Ganges in the Garhwal: Badrinath, Jamunotri, Kedarnath and Gangotri.

To reach any of these sources by the conventional route upriver is hard enough, for each lies in the High Himalaya. Every year, villagers from the Indian plains make the pilgrimages to these sites, often with inadequate clothing and considerable personal suffering. Having visited one site, they go back downriver to a confluence with another tributary so that they can make their way upstream to the next source.

But the true Hindu devotees (and I loved the affectionate way Indians pronounced this as '*devo-tees*'), the *sadhus*, take the pilgrimage a stage further. They traverse directly across the mountains from one pilgrimage site to another along the *yatra* trails, a journey across the roof of the world that demanded every inch of Shipton's and Tilman's legendary toughness, but which many *sadhus* undertake in sandals.

I had once arrived in Kedarnath at the start of the pilgrimage season, on 1 May, when the town had just been reoccupied after its winter hibernation. It had been an extraordinary sight, like an apparition that one of the early sixth-century Chinese travellers might have stumbled across as they made those first tortuous crossings of the Himalaya: a large temple at the centre of a tight bowl of Himalayan mountains, with simple wooden houses radiating out from it.

Eight feet of snow was being cleared from the narrow streets in front of the temple. A young boy, stripped to the waist as a penance and shivering with cold, was ringing the temple bell for *aarti*; the sound echoed around the mountain bowl with monotonous intensity.

Some of the wildest figures I had ever seen lined the temple compound: *naga sadhus*, the warrior 'Hell's Angels' of the Hindu world, with long matted hair and ash-smeared bodies, who view themselves as outcasts from conventional society, like Shiva, the dark, wild god of the Hindu pantheon, often pictured brooding in his retreat in the Himalaya.

Many of the *naga sadhus* remained all year at this altitude, taking the *yatra* trails or crossing over to Tibet, being as disdainful of international frontiers as they are of most human restrictions. A group of them wearing reflective dark glasses, like rock stars, stared down at me intimidatingly as I passed.

Entering the temple, I took off my boots to walk on the sodden, freezing flagstones. In the half-light provided by the flickering candles and the low-wattage red bulbs, I could make out Shiva, and a *lingam* at the end of a passage, in glimpses made fleeting by the press of pilgrims both ahead of me and behind me as we filed around the narrow walkway. The pilgrims were craning their necks to see these images, for in Hinduism the act of *darshan*, of seeing a deity, is in itself beneficial.

Later I talked to the boy who had been ringing the bell. He was twenty-one, but had already done seven years of penance by keeping his leg immobile in a sling. When the doctors examined his withered leg at the end of this time, they feared he would lose it. However, his older *sadhu* mentor advised him that massage would bring back feeling to the leg, as indeed it had done, although it still looked painfully frail. I met other *sadhus* there who had also taken extreme ascetic vows, such as remaining silent for many years.

Yet almost more moving was the spirituality of those who were now coming up from the valley below – the villagers of the Indian plains, many of whom had never seen snow before, let alone a mountain, and who were wrapped in thin blue plastic sheets to keep out the snow and the rain; each year, many die of exposure. They had come to have *darshan* of the images inside the Kedarnath temple.

I felt humbled by the intensity of their faith that had brought them this high and made them this vulnerable. An elderly man stopped to tell me his story. He had once been a farmer. Then at sixty-two he had become a *sannyasi*, sold his land and left his family, in an attempt to find salvation without worldly possessions. Now he was seventy-five and coming to Kedarnath for the first time. As he told me this, his eyes filled with tears. 'I would be happy to die here,' he said. He had a tiny lingam-shaped pebble that he kept in a cup, inside a casket. He now showed it to me – a keepsake, or treasure in the real sense, which he kept close to him to give him comfort.

Likewise at Gangotri, considered by many to be the true source of the Ganges, I had seen the river issue directly from the mouth of a glacier called 'the cow's mouth', within sight of the pyramidal spire of Shivling, 'Shiva's peak'. It was even colder than at Kedarnath and again I was accompanied by a few Indian pilgrims, shivering in thin woollen blankets as they muttered prayers to themselves.

So I was aware how suffused this land was with a spiritual charge. The four principal tributaries of the Ganges spread their net right across the Garhwal. As the tributaries descended from their respective sources, they meet each other at holy towns called prayags, with what is considered a redoubling of spiritual force. And where the Ganges bursts out as a uniform whole onto the plain below, at Hardwar, I had once seen the Kumbh Mela festival, which takes place every twelve years and is considered the largest religious gathering in the world.

Early at dawn on the principal day of that Kumbh Mela, I had climbed up onto a tenement rooftop high above the river. Far below, half a million people were trying to get into the water at the auspicious time, with little boats of marigolds being cast onto the fast-flowing Ganges. The tents of the Vaishnavite and Shaivite *sadhus* stretched in all directions and I felt like an angel as I looked down on this sea of spirituality from a great height. One curious effect was that the only smell that seemed to rise up this high from the streets and river below was the ritual incense. Everything else – the smell of food, animals, excrement and traffic so familiar in Indian small-town life – had been filtered out, leaving the incense alone to rise to the skies.

Not far upriver from our own bathing place, we came to the first of the holy towns where the Ganges divides, Devra Prayag. As we drove on up the circuitous gorge that our tributary of the river, the Alaknanda, had carved above Devra Prayag, I was continually reminded that we were passing through a holy landscape, with signs to villages that I had visited like Triyugi Narayan or Gauri Kund, places associated with Hindu legend, especially Shiva.

I thought of the arrogance of the early British travellers to Nanda Devi who seemed not to have noticed the count-less Indian pilgrims going the same way, an arrogance occasionally mirrored by their modern successors who assume that only they, as foreigners, appreciate the mountains. Shipton and Tilman were honourable exceptions to this; Tilman in particular had been constantly aware of the spiritual regard in which Nanda Devi was held.

The source we were travelling to, of the Rishi Ganges in the Nanda Devi Sanctuary, was as venerated as those of other tributaries of the Ganges, but not as a place of pilgrimage for the common man. As the name suggests, this was a retreat that could only be reached by 'Rishis', the mythical enlightened sages of Hindu legend who were thought to be halfway to God, and so able to reach such an inaccessible spot. Mere mortals could never attempt it.

I had once come across a parable about Nanda Devi told

by Swami Rama-Krishna, an Indian mystic who lived in Rishikesh, which played on this idea:

> The seeker, the Rishi, climbs up the valley where 'the Ganges falls like a flight of stairs let down for the sons of man' till he reaches a mountain so high that it is always in cloud [Nanda Devi]; he climbs up the edge of this frosty cirrus; still no Heaven! He rants and raves to God at the treachery of it all, but, getting no response, sits down to brood. Far below he sees the world, which he had found wanting. It seems now so fresh and clear and full of unbounded joy, where previously it had been so closed with walls that hid so much. He understood now why God must be wise, for he lives with the perspective of the world. He begins to descend, but God appears and says he cannot now rejoin the world of men.

*

As a cameraman whom I once worked with used to say, there was 'plenty of the old left hand, right hand' as we swung around the canyon bends, past the various signs that had been put up to encourage careful driving: 'Life is short. Don't make it shorter'; 'If you love her, divorce speed'; 'Death lays his icy hands on speed kings.'

A steady stream of pilgrims were making their way up to the various temples by foot, alongside the road, but I felt no guilt at being in a bus – there would be quite enough walking later. For a road high up in the mountains, it was in surprisingly good condition. This was not through any desire of the Indian Government's to encourage coachloads of pilgrims, but to allow the rapid deployment of troops to the border with Tibet in the event of any Chinese hostility. 'We were caught with our pants down in 1962,' an Indian friend had once told me, and military sensitivity over the border was still acute.

The river-gorge was so deep that there were palm trees growing at the bottom in the microclimate it created. From our bus I could look down to see little hand-operated river pulleys across it, just as in the Andes, while in the distance were the first looming mountains, the outrunners of the High Himalaya beyond.

We came to Rudraprayag, the next division of the rivers, where pilgrims head either to the shrine of Kedarnath or that of Badrinath. For me it was a place of pilgrimage in itself, as this was where Jim Corbett had killed the celebrated 'man-eating leopard of Rudraprayag'.

The story is almost forgotten now, but at the time it was a worldwide sensation. Between 1918 and 1926, a single leopard killed more than 125 people around Rudraprayag, a staggering statistic that must make it one of the most prolific serial killers in history.

The attacks had begun during the worldwide Spanish Flu epidemic of 1918. The epidemic claimed the lives of 1 million people in India. In Garhwal, the death toll was such that the hill people, rather than cremate their dead in the customary Hindu way, placed a burning coal in the mouths of the corpses and left them outside the villages to decompose.

A leopard began to scavenge these corpses and soon acquired a taste for human flesh, a taste that, with few guns in the local population, it could develop with relative impunity among the flimsy village huts.

By the time Jim Corbett arrived, in 1925, a blind terror had descended on the villages, provoked not just by the sheer number of leopard killings but by the savagery with which they were carried out. Nor was it just the local population who were at risk. Because Rudraprayag lies on two major pilgrimage routes, an estimated 60,000 travellers passed through the leopard's territory each spring. Despite the pilgrims' vulnerability to attack, as they often camped out in the open, it is a measure of their faith that numbers do not appear to have fallen during those years.

On one occasion a group of twenty pilgrims, on their way, like us, towards Badrinath, found themselves at nightfall near a small roadside shop here and asked the shopkeeper if they could sleep on an open platform beside it. The shopkeeper begged them to carry on a few miles to some pilgrim shelters, but they were too tired. A *sadhu* joined them and claimed that he would in any case be a match for any leopard, so while the women slept in the small shop, the men and the *sadhu* bedded down outside.

The *sadhu* slept in the middle of all the men, as befitted their protector. When the others awoke in the morning, they found that he had been killed silently in the night by the leopard and his body dragged across three fields, before being eaten.

After a while, sheer panic seems to have affected the local population's ability to deal with the animal. They

The Alaknanda Ganges: *'In the distance were the first looming mountains, the outrunners of the High Himalaya.'*

Hindu pilgrims celebrating *aarti* near Rishikesh: *'the Garhwal was a land suffused with a spiritual charge'*.

'A rainbow appeared, neatly spanning the Dhaoli Ganges.'

Steve Berry: 'He reminded me of a member of one of the sixties bands he so admired; a rocker who had been on the road a long time but who still kept a bit of rebellious rock and roll flickering away underneath it all.'

Above Lata.

The untouched forests of the Sanctuary.

Dewan Singh Butola, a porter on Shipton
and Tilman's expeditions in the 1930s.

Inside the Nanda Devi Sanctuary at twilight.

A rare glimpse of Changabang, 'the shining mountain', from within the Sanctuary.

Above Cairns marking the entrance to the Sanctuary. *Below* 'We would occasionally get glimpses of Nanda Devi, but often it would be hidden by the gorge or cloud. This was the way you got to know a mountain, from different angles, obliquely and with respect.'

George Band, with the outer 'curtain wall' behind him: *'He had the loping, slightly bow-legged gait of a man who has been rolling down from summits all his life.'*

John Shipton collecting seeds on the slopes above Lata.

Trisul: for many years after 1907 the highest mountain ever climbed; Bull skied down it.

Colonel Narinder 'Bull' Kumar: *'People spend their entire lives wanting just one of the little medals I wear on the third row down.'*

NEXT PAGE

Nanda Devi with the Rishi Ganges below.

were superstitious at the best of times, but in the leopard they felt they had encountered a fiend incarnate. On one occasion they surrounded it in a cave but failed to secure the entrance properly, and so the leopard escaped over the heads of the terrified crowd.

When Corbett arrived to deal with the problem in 1925, he already had a considerable reputation as a tiger-killer. He knew the hills well and had some trusted men with him. He was also a renowned shot.

But in the leopard he faced a formidable adversary. By now it had become used to the ways of men and was unusually cunning. An older male, it was strong and could carry the body of its victims for long distances; its hunting ground extended for some 500 square miles around Rudraprayag.

Corbett was able to get close to the leopard on several occasions, but was prevented each time from killing it by bad weather or the leopard's instinctive caution. Resorting to poison, he found that the leopard seemed impervious even to cyanide. He was dismayed both by his own failure and the death toll, which continued to mount around him. After each new death, he agonised that he was responsible. And the leopard very nearly killed him too; on several occasions he found the leopard's distinctive pug-marks in the sand of a path and realised that he was the one who had been stalked the previous night; once the leopard leapt over a thorn-bush enclosure within which he was sleeping.

Corbett's tracking skills were superb: he could build an artificial *maidan*, lay gun- and gin-traps, even imitate the leopard's call and attract the man-eater to him. A skilled naturalist, he was particularly adept at letting the birds and animals of the forest lead him to the leopard by their alarm calls.

Yet the most distinctive feature of Corbett's account of the chase, *The Man-Eating Leopard of Rudraprayag* (1947), is its relentlessness. The long months of stalking and sleepless nights begin to take on a mesmeric, dreamlike intensity. At one point Corbett describes the leopard as moving below his hideout with a sound 'like the soft rustle of a woman's dress'. He sinks into tunnel vision as he tries to get the leopard in his sights, his days punctuated only by reports of further deaths brought to him by hill people who continually expect him to ease their burden.

It is this obsessive quality that makes *The Man-Eating Leopard of Rudraprayag* a classic in the literature of the chase, along with Household's *Rogue Male* and Harris's *The Silence of the Lambs*. And the leopard seems to rival Hannibal Lecter in the cruelty and refinement of its killings.

Like those other classics of the chase, there is a caesura in the middle when the pursuit is halted, only for the participants to re-engage with even greater viciousness after the break. In late 1925, Corbett retreated to his home in distant Naini Tal, exhausted by the long nights spent waiting for the leopard and beaten by the onset of winter. Then he returned the following spring, just as the largest number of pilgrims began to enter the hills.

The leopard had grown yet more daring. In a stunningly audacious and cruel kill, the man-eater strolled into the heart of a village in daylight, lay under some steps as if it were a dog and seized a young boy as he returned home from a well. Dislocating the boy's head with one twist, it carried the corpse out of the village and across three fields, before consuming it.

Corbett was greeted by the boy's mother with the heart-rending cry: 'What crime, Parmeswhar, has my son, who was loved by all, committed that on the threshold of life he has deserved death in this terrible way?'

Corbett waited for many more nights but, although he heard accounts of the leopard's activities elsewhere, did not see him. He decided it was time to leave. On the eve of his departure, a large party of 150 pilgrims were spending the night in one of the shelters. Corbett felt it was an opportunity to have one last try. He waited in a tree near by and, just in case the pilgrims were not a sufficient bait, staked a live goat out in the open.

The leopard was attracted to the area by the pilgrims' lights. Corbett was unsure whether it would go for the pilgrims or the goat first. It went for the goat. He turned his torch on, saw the leopard and shot. The torch went out at that moment, so he did not know whether he had hit the man-eater, nor did he dare descend the tree in the darkness to check.

In the morning he found the leopard's body. It had the distinctive pug-markings of the man-eater. But, says Corbett, in defeat it had shrunk: 'here was only an old leopard, who differed from others of his kind in that his muzzle was grey and his lips lacked whiskers; the best hated and the most feared animal in all India'.

It is Jim Corbett's humanity in the face of the leopard's onslaught that impresses, and his deep affection for the people of the hills: a favourite scene that punctuates many of the long chase sequences is of Corbett sitting in the shade of a mango tree and gathering intelligence from the locals as they all drink tea.

Those who deplore Corbett as a big-gun hunter – perhaps why his book has been so forgotten – overlook the fact that he was far from being a gratuitous killer; he went on to become a keen conservationist and to found the Indian National Park that bears his name.

There was a plaque on the tree that he had used for his final stake-out of the leopard and I drank a cup of chai from a local stallholder in his honour, before departing.

*

That evening, as we drove higher up the Ganges, I saw a line of single trees silhouetted like sentinels by the evening sun along the ridgeline of the gorge. I thought of Corbett's words about these hills: 'Darkness when used in connection with night is a relative term and has no fixed standard.' The long indeterminate twilight of the Himalaya often afforded the clearest vision. We passed a small *stupa*-like building where a group of *sadhus* had lit a fire and were huddled around it, their dreadlocks moving in front of the flame like snakes.

We went through small roadside settlements, many of them places I had stayed in before. I liked the way in which a *tableau vivant* could be glimpsed briefly in each of the shacks as the bus flashed by: a man being shaved by a red electric light; a family clustered around a STD booth, trying to make a call to some remittance man down on the plains; a bored middle-aged shopkeeper swatting flies away from his array of magic tricks and toys; a jabbering group of men around a *karim* board, the game that is a cross between shove ha'penny and pool, and is played fast and loose in the Garhwal.

I remembered the intense shock of the red jacaranda trees flowering against the green of the hills when I had come here in spring and how the wild white roses draped themselves languorously over branches like great canopies, with a scent that filled the twilight.

Finally, as the sky turned an indolent indigo-violet and the trucks started coming at us with their horns and flashing headlights, I saw the lights of Joshimath ahead in the distance, our jumping-off point for the expedition proper, and my adrenaline started to rise.

*

My Indian pilgrim's guidebook stated: 'In Joshimath you will find every facility (Telephone, Telegraph and Banking) available to the traveller.' At first sight it seemed more like a Wild West town, with dusty streets crisscrossed by telegraph wires and shacks selling toilet paper, sandals, pilgrims' staffs and torches.

There were also many small hostels for the travellers going further up-river to the head of the Alaknanda Ganges and the shrine at Badrinath; in winter, when their own temple-town became uninhabitable, the priests from that shrine brought the images down to Joshimath for greater safety, so they were sister towns, each with their own holy buildings.

Badrinath was a reminder that the sources of the Ganges had been pilgrimage sites for the Buddhists long before they had been for the Hindus. In the temple at Badrinath there was even a statue of Vishnu sitting in the classic cross-legged *padmasan* posture of the Buddha; it looks like a Buddhist statue that was simply reconsecrated as Vishnu by the ever-pragmatic Hindus when they expelled their rivals.

The man who led the expulsion of the Buddhists and was largely responsible for the creation of the Hindu pilgrimage tradition was one of the most remarkable in India's history. Variously hailed as the Indian Aquinas or Luther, Adiguru Shankaracharya was a controversial figure. Born about AD 790 in Kerala in the far south of India, Shankara (as he is usually known) is credited with revitalising Hinduism after a long period when India had been dominated by Buddhism. He managed to strip away some of the over-elaborate rituals of the Brahmins, while incorporating the more popular aspects of Buddhist thought. Hinduism was reborn as a vibrant, popular religion.

Shankara was a traveller of prodigious energy. He created four great *maths* or monasteries, and located them at the four points of the compass in India: one in his home region of Mysore in the south, one on the west coast at Ouri, one on the east coast at Dvaraka – and the most spectacularly positioned of all, this one in the far north, below the snows of Badrinath.

Pilgrimages had previously been a Buddhist tradition, but Shankara incorporated them into Hindu thinking and stressed the importance of the Himalaya as a sacred place, 'the abode of Shiva'. He was greatly drawn to the mountains. At Kedarnath, I had seen the statue of him on the slopes above the temple, advancing yet further up into the hills, holding a staff, ice axe and water bottle.

The statue is there because this is traditionally where he had disappeared into the mountains, aged just thirty-two. He was never seen again. I had always found it moving that this young, able man of such enormous physical and intellectual energy, who had taken his ideas right across the whole of India, debating and proselytising in Sanskrit as he went, should have died in the snows at such a young age.

Yet there were ambiguities about Shankara as well. The expulsion of the Buddhists from India was accomplished with a Lutheran vigour that often caused bloodshed, although Hindu tradition sometimes pretends that it was done peacefully. The Hindus appropriated the Buddhist traditions that had been most popular – those of pilgrimage, for instance – and built over many Buddhist sites, as they have tried to do more recently with some mosques.

Whilst the spiritual home of Buddhism became Tibet, there were still many traces of it in these Indian hills, the glacial remains of the faith as it retreated beyond the Himalaya.

*

I went with Loreto McNaught-Davis to try to find the Shankaracharya shrine in Joshimath, or rather one of them, for such was the reverence in which he was held that three rival denominations had built monasteries in his honour.

Loreto was the only member of the party interested enough in the Hindu heartland to join me. I was pleased, as she was excellent company, having all the charm of a worldly Chilean who had travelled widely. Mac liked to tease her about the elegant clothes she wore to the hills, but despite the Hermès scarves, she was a tough and resourceful traveller who had accompanied him on some demanding treks. It was also good, if incongruous, to be speaking Spanish in the middle of the Himalaya.

We made our way through the maze of competing temples in honour of Shankara. At the lowest and smallest of them, an ancient tree in the courtyard had been wrapped around in layers of red string by Hindu pilgrims, each of whom had added another strand; the result looked like an Ayurvedic spider's web circling around a tree of faith.

We were contemplating the tree, as we thought alone, when a loud voice assailed us: 'Excuse me, sir and madam, can I help you?' An unusual figure was standing behind the tree in an overgrown garden full of marigolds and nemesia, smiling and beaming through thick black-rimmed glasses and wearing what looked suspiciously like a Beatles toupee. It was clear that whether we wanted him to or not, he was going to help us anyway. Mr Chandra introduced himself as the self-appointed guardian of the tree. 'I loved this place so much that when I came, I stayed. I am at that time of life, you see. The time when a man can take *sannyas*.'

I was used to the idea of *sannyasi* as those men of a certain age who abjured family, business and the trappings of their previous existence to seek salvation and quiet in the last stages of life, like the pilgrim I had met in Kedarnath. But Mr Chandra, while undoubtedly devout, was anything but quiet. Loreto and I found ourselves in the teeth of a monologist of formidable stamina.

'Ah yes, I lived forty years in London, forty years – when I started there I was in a small apartment off the Earls Court Road, it was rotten, really rotten, with no light and the water seeping down, but by the time I finished I had a Seiko watch and a Jaguar XJ6, well, several cars actually' (he listed them all) 'but the Jaguar was the last. I had become a "*chartered account-ant*", oh yes, I made a few bob, but then I quit and I was living in Kerala and I came to Joshimath on pilgrimage.'

The stream of consciousness stopped for a moment as he paused and got out his asthma inhaler: 'When the sun is out, and with the dust on the marigolds, I sometimes get it – now where was I? Yes I came to Joshimath on pilgrimage and visited this shrine of Adiguru Shankaracharya – he came from Kerala too, you know – and decided to stay. I built this little hut and planted this garden. And here I am.'

Sensing he had created a moment's pause, he quickly plunged on: 'Now Buddha, of course, probably you are thinking of him.' He peered at us suspiciously, as if we must be like the other feckless Westerners he had to deal with. 'He was actually a Hindu, an avatar of Vishnu. He read the Vedas and realised they made sense. And actually, he copied them.

'Do you know what zero means? It means infinite and worthless. And that is where Buddhism leads you. Did you know, they do not believe in a God? Absolutely not. They see no need for a book either – but we Hindus do. We have a need for a creator. We are open. Whatever little you have, enjoy.' Mr Chandra opened his arms towards us and seemed to want to draw us deeper into the marigolds with him. 'We welcome all religions.'

The welcome that Hinduism gives to all other religions is usually that of the spider to the fly; it absorbs and syncretises their essence. The Hindu ambivalence towards Buddhism comes from a strong sense that, while they notionally tried to include it within the fold in the usual Hindu absorbent way, it was too atheistic, too beyond the pale, too onanistic. It was a threat. And so Shankara and the other Hindu reformers of the first millennium successfully banished it to Tibet.

Mr Chandra insisted that we go inside his hut to look at his photographs of London, of his cars and of Earls Court. But Loreto, with a diplomatic charm I could not have managed, laid a perfumed hand on his shoulder and said: 'Mr Chandra, we would so much like to hear more of your stories. But we have to go and climb a mountain.'

*

The whole group walked up the mountain behind Joshimath, to the meadows at Auli, to get our first view of Nanda Devi in the distance. It was an impressive sight as it towered beyond the meadow and the forest, massive and serene.

With the foreshortening of perspective, and alpine flowers in the foreground, the famous profile of the summit looked statuesque, rather than savage, and the fearsome gorge was hidden. Lest we got complacent, George Band pointed out the buttress below the summit where an American expedition had ended in tragedy in 1976.

As it was, a febrile air of nervous concern about the climb had already descended over the group. We had just heard that the Indo-Tibetan Border Police had mounted an expedition into the Sanctuary and was attempting the peak. The Indo-Tibetan Border Police (or ITBP) was a quasi-military outfit that had been formed after the Indo-China War to protect the border better.

The ITBP expedition was good news in that as it would be the first to go into the Sanctuary for such a long time, it would have to reopen the pathways and lay log bridges across the Rishi Ganges. Less good was that one of the team members had already died and the group had radioed military headquarters, asking for permission to get out.

This last intelligence came via Akshay Kumar, Bull's son, who was accompanying our expedition. Compared to the colonel, Akshay was very much new-generation Indian – Ray-Bans, fashionably shaved head, *bhangra* music – but he had inherited some of his father's tough attitude: 'Of course the IMF [the Indian Mountaineering

Federation] told them, "Just because one man's died, that doesn't mean that you can't keep on with the attempt." I mean, what the bloody hell did they expect?'

I talked to him as we wandered back down to Josh-imath. Akshay had ambivalent feelings about the mountains, understandable given that his own brother had died in a climbing accident and his father Bull had suffered more close calls than most. He also told me of the tragic Indian expedition to Everest in 1985, which had wiped out the cream of the country's mountaineers, including his uncle, Kiran Kumar.

Akshay preferred rafting and had led the first expedition down the uncharted waters of the Upper Brahmaputra. He had come with us to help his father coordinate the formidable amount of logistics needed for our assault on the Sanctuary.

When we got back to Joshimath, Akshay, Bull, Steve Berry and John Shipton huddled over their maps, planning the approach route. John, normally so laid back, now appeared worried. The problem was that none of our party, including the porters, had taken our particular approach route before. But then the owner of our hotel, B.S. Rana, mentioned that he had been a member of almost the last expedition to get into the Sanctuary, in 1981. Rana had been the cook and could point out precisely the best routes and campsites. More disturbingly, he also mentioned that five members of that 1981 expedition had died.

I had by now at least learnt everybody's name on our own expedition. In addition to the various leaders – John Shipton, Bull, Steve Berry – and Mac, Loreto, Akshay and

George Band, there was Natalena Dacunha, the computer specialist from Holland; David Baber and David Sayer, two jovial and experienced British trekkers; Gerald Becker, a wiry American; Alan Tate, an expert potholer; Albert Chapman and Howard Humphreys, from a Yorkshire climbing club; and two friends from the Midlands, Jeff Ford and Barry Bond, who were extremely fit and had been on several expeditions before.

Mac sat me down over a beer that he had somehow managed to get smuggled into the hotel. He had the politician's knack of making you feel that he had chosen you, and you alone, to take into his confidence: 'Hugh, I'm worried. There are a lot of us. We're already a large party – seventeen. You know they've now asked us to take two more Indian liaison officers – one from the IMF, one from the Forestry Department. I mean, it's fucking ridiculous. We'll have at least fifty porters. I mean, are we part of the solution or part of the fucking problem?'

As President of the International Mountaineering and Climbing Federation, Mac had been asked to write a feasibility report on whether the Sanctuary should be opened again to the wider mountaineering world (the ITBP expedition being a strictly local and military visit). Mac was aware that a lot was riding on this report. Although the Indian Government were letting us in, this didn't mean that they would let in anyone else. His recommendations would be critical in persuading the government to open up the Sanctuary in an ecologically sustainable way, if this were possible.

Clearly what was called for was a policy of low-impact,

low-intensity mountaineering, with small groups paying large fees to help the local community and the environment – but at the moment we were turning into the sort of large expedition that would have had Eric Shipton turning in his grave. It was large expeditions 'trashing' the Sanctuary that had, I gathered, been the reason for closing it in the first place.

Nor was that Mac's only concern: 'This isn't going to be a picnic. Have you read Shipton's account of going up the gorge?' I had, but a long time ago and not when I ever dreamt I might be doing it myself. 'Well, it was tough going. Are all our team up to it' – at this point he laid a hand on my arm – 'including you?'

This was a question I'd been asking myself for the past week. Although I'd spent a great deal of time in every mountain range on the planet, I was not a mountaineer of the rope, tooth and nail variety, and didn't claim to be. When I'd reminded Steve of this before departure, he had waved it airily aside: 'As long as you've got a good head for heights, you'll be fine.' As I was later to discover, this was in the 'if you can manage a length in the pool, you can swim the Channel' league of understatement.

My suspicions had been aroused when Steve had told me: 'Of course, you'll need to bring a climbing harness, a helmet and a jumar.'

'I thought I didn't need any of that stuff,' I'd protested.

'Ah well,' said Steve vaguely, 'I've been reading a bit more about the gorge. Worth bringing, just in case.'

In the frenzy of getting everything for departure, I had let this ride. But now that we had a little time, I thought I had better reread Shipton's and Tilman's respective accounts of their expeditions to the Nanda Devi Sanctuary, and of the Rishi Ganges gorge that was the only possible way into it.

Temperamentally Shipton and his partner Tilman could not have been more different. The photo of the two of them leaving for Nanda Devi shows this. Shipton is wearing a dapper double-breasted suit and is clean-shaven with dishevelled wavy hair. He could be mistaken for Stephen Spender (and indeed Spender's brother was an accomplished contemporary mountaineer, who later explored with Shipton, as did the brothers of W.H. Auden and Graham Greene). In his previous life as a coffee planter in Kenya's Happy Valley, Shipton had been celebrated as a good dancer. He belonged to the twenties and thirties set for whom experimentation in travel, sex and literature was natural.

By comparison Tilman, with his military moustache, is burlier and looks set in his ways. Crucially, he was of the older generation who had fought in the First World War. A man of few words and fixed views, Tilman was the antithesis of his companion, Shipton, who made the point with an anecdote about their respective waking times: 'I have never met anyone with such a complete disregard for the sublime comforts of the early morning bed. However monstrously early we might decide, the night before, to get up, he was about at least half an hour before the time.' And while Shipton had a notoriously wandering eye for women, Tilman was equally known for a bachelor attitude bordering on misogyny.

But whatever their differences, or perhaps because of them, they formed one of the most effective exploring combinations of all time. They refused to be beaten by the terrors of the gorge during the months of their assault on it. My respect for both them and the gorge that we were going to attempt was heightened when I became attuned to their self-deprecating language. For Shipton to say: 'The gorge wore a grim and desolate aspect . . . I found myself to be nervous and shaky . . . it looked to be utterly impassable . . . my heart was in my mouth,' was quite something, given his usual British reticence.

After all, this was the way in which he had ended his account of their adventures together on Nanda Devi: 'As we had done in Africa, we continued to address one another as "Tilman" and "Shipton"; and when, after seven months continuously together, I suggested that it was time he called me "Eric", he became acutely embarrassed, hung his head and muttered, "It sounds so damned silly." '

Their achievement – in getting up the gorge to become the first human beings to set foot in the Sanctuary – was extraordinary and was rightly recognised as such by the climbing world. Shipton and Tilman made their reputations with their cracking of the Nanda Devi puzzle, perhaps the great success story of British pre-war mountaineering.

Two years later, in 1936, Tilman returned to Nanda Devi, without Shipton but with an Anglo-American team that included Charles Houston and Noël Odell.

Tilman led his party back along the Rishi Ganges gorge

and into the Sanctuary, along the route that Shipton and he had discovered. Once the Sanctuary had been breached, the actual climb to the top of Nanda Devi was not technically difficult (Shipton and Tilman had correctly worked out the easiest ascent route in 1934) but it was still testing for the two lead summiteers, Noël Odell and Tilman himself.

So strong was the team's ethos that on their return they agreed not to reveal who had reached the summit, claiming it as an 'expedition effort'. However, the press, eager for a British success after all the failures on Everest, managed to coax the information out of them. Tilman's and Odell's ascent to the summit of Nanda Devi in 1936 was a solace to the British for that failure to climb Everest. For some fifteen years afterwards, Nanda Devi remained the highest mountain ever climbed in the world.

Both Shipton and Tilman wrote accounts of their exploration and climbs, which have become classics: Shipton's *Nanda Devi* (1936) was his first and in some ways freshest book, full of a wide-eyed idealism and illustrated with charming woodcuts; Tilman's *The Ascent of Nanda Devi* (1938) is written in a more restrained style, as might be expected, but it has some quiet strengths and a dry sense of humour about his American climbing colleagues.

Tilman describes how on the top of Nanda Devi, Odell and he enjoyed uncharacteristic sunshine and a clear view over towards Tibet. Elated by the climb, Tilman comments: 'I believe we so far forgot ourselves as to shake hands on it.'

More reflectively, he pondered on the descent: 'I

remember, in the small hours when the spark of life burns lowest, the feeling which predominated over all was one of remorse at the fall of a giant. It is the same sort of contrition that one feels at the shooting of an elephant.'

*

I was sharing a bedroom with George Band. The noise of Indian pilgrims celebrating outside, with the occasional firework, kept us awake and we talked for some time, despite an intended early start for the mountains the next day.

He told me of going to Everest in 1953 as the youngest member of John Hunt's expedition, although he had never climbed in the Himalaya before: 'But I'd been lucky and just had a very good season in the Alps. So when they wanted an extra climber from both Cambridge and Oxford, I was put forward as the Cambridge University choice.'

I was fascinated by the details he told me of the Everest trip – how for instance John Hunt, always meticulous about the expedition equipment, had asked that possum fur was used to line their boots. Hunt had been chosen for precisely that grasp of organisational detail. Mindful of the French experience on Annapurna a few years earlier, when the glory of their successful ascent had been tarnished by Herzog's severe frostbite, Hunt had also replaced the usual hobnailed soles, which gripped well but conducted the cold, with rubber Dunlop ones.

But the essentials of mountaineering equipment had not changed that much over the years. Both George and I had seen a recent film documentary showing the recovery of George Mallory's body from Everest, seventy-five years after he'd disappeared heading up the north-east ridge. Aside from the tasteless publicising of the corpse, what had struck us both was the intelligent layering of Mallory's clothing, and how well the natural materials would have worked.

I asked George about Eric Shipton, whom he'd known; indeed, Shipton had very nearly led the 1953 Everest expedition and had only been replaced, controversially, by Hunt at a late stage.

As George reminded me, since 1933 Shipton had been involved in almost all the previous reconnaissances of Everest. By 1953, he was generally accepted to be the best mountaineer of his generation. An outsider might have thought Shipton would have been shoehorned into the job of leading the British team to Everest. But the outsider would have reckoned without the Alpine Club.

The stakes were high. The French had already climbed Annapurna in 1950, the first of the 8,000-metre peaks to fall. Nineteen fifty-three would be the last year for some time that the British would have a window to climb Everest – 1954 would undoubtedly be allocated to another nation.

The old men in their armchairs, who formed the Joint Himalayan Committee and picked the Everest teams, had never quite got over the feeling that Eric was a bit suspect: a man who liked working at close quarters with Sherpas; a man who liked to boast that he had never owned a home and never would; a man who was a 'free spirit'.

What was needed (one almost hears them saying it) was 'a safe pair of hands' – in this case John Hunt, who had much less climbing experience and was not particularly fit, but who had a genius for logistics. For the plan was that this was to be a classic siege campaign, conducted with a series of camps and an army of porters, far from the lightweight, more intuitive approach that Shipton liked to take.

At first they suggested that Hunt join Shipton as a 'co-leader'. This was not such a bad idea, as their qualities would have complemented one another well. But something in the way that this was put to Shipton made him bridle, tact not being high on the Alpine Club's list of attributes.

Eric Shipton refused to go. Some of his mountaineering friends backed him by threatening to withdraw from the expedition. Hunt's subsequent recomposition of the team gave a chance to less-experienced reserves – men, in fact, like the young George Band, who, as he himself pointed out, had never previously been to the Himalaya.

At first Shipton withdrew to his tent and sulked. It was a slight from which his friends thought he would never fully recover. He had, after all, been the first to see and reconnoitre the route by which Everest would eventually be climbed: the south-western approach beyond the fearsome Khumbu ice fall, which had been considered impassable even by close associates such as Tilman.

Shipton had argued that it was possible, and went there in 1951 to prove it. With him on the slopes of Kala Patar, when he first saw that there was a way up the South Col, was a young and unknown New Zealand mountaineer, a bee-keeper by the name of Edmund Hillary, whom Shipton had invited to join him.

It is hard to imagine how Shipton must have felt when Hillary took that same route two years later in 1953 and conquered Everest without him, together with Tenzing Norgay, whom Shipton had also introduced to the mountain.

However, he was not someone to bear a grudge. It is a measure of the man that he went to meet John Hunt, Hillary, George Band and the other returning heroes when they flew back to England, even inviting them all to stay with him.

George added mischievously: 'Of course when he was in India, Eric slung his ice axe beside many a memsahib's bed. Famous for it. Can't say I knew him well, though. Not sure many people did.'

By now George and I had now been talking in the dark for some time, like two kids after lights out. The Hindu pilgrims were still letting off fireworks in the street with the raucous Indian fondness for maximum noise and violence. I finally fell asleep with the sound of Garhwali revellers celebrating into the small hours.

The next morning I was not at my best, nor was I cheered by George: 'A funny thing happened last night. I woke up, looked across at you as you lay asleep and there was a shaft of moonlight coming in from outside. Your face was very pale. You looked exactly like Mallory's corpse when they found him. It gave me quite a shock.'

It was not what I wanted to hear as we were about to begin the expedition.

*

We were heading deeper into the Garhwal, so we needed to repack, leaving any unnecessary kit behind at the hotel. In my case this was an operation that demanded considerable concentration. I had left Britain in a hurry, with only a few weeks between signing up for the expedition and getting on a plane. The simplest technique had been to throw every conceivable object into a bag and leave decisions until later.

Now I whittled things down to a few shirts and the bare necessities. I couldn't claim the austerity of a Shipton or a Tilman, but it looked respectably restrained. I did have one indulgence, however: on the flight over I'd told the Scandinavian Airlines air hostess that I was heading for a temperance zone and great discomfort, and she had presented me with a full tray of Absolut Vodka miniatures. There were twenty-eight of them. I laced these through the kitbag so that the search for socks or a fleece would at least be enlivened by the occasional hit of a plastic bottle. I had also brought a Walkman, as I knew there were moments when only the complete oblivion of music would do, and just hoped the Alpine Club would never find out.

My photographic equipment was more daunting. I had a tripod and a Pelikan case full of camera bodies and lenses. Akshay had arranged for a local lad to help me carry all this extra gear on the trek. At about twenty-two, quick and able, Bishen Singh looked as if he would be the ideal assistant and as we travelled up the valley to the little village of Lata, the jumping-off point for Nanda Devi, I took him through the equipment.

We began to gain altitude. Lata was at 8,000 feet, perched high above the river. The fields around it were full of yellow mustard seed. The village itself seemed a cheerful community from the outside, spread over the hill, its slate roofs covered with red chillies and bales of drying hay. Shipton had written of it: 'Life in these little mountain villages is delightfully simple, and the inhabitants are almost all self-supporting' – but a little poking around showed that it was a far from happy place. And while Shipton might describe it as 'delightfully simple', it's unclear whether this was as delightful for the inhabitant as for the onlooker.

Nehru once wrote: 'The dominant impression one retains of the Garhwal is one of isolation and poverty. It is extraordinary to be so near and yet so far from the rest of the world.'

This was the homeland of the Bhotia people. Like mountain people the world over, they had always fought sturdily for their independence from the plains below. The great Mughal Empires of India had never beaten them. The first invaders to conquer them had come not from the plain, but from neighbouring Nepal – the Gurkhas, who took possession briefly at the end of the eighteenth century. The British annexed the area in 1815 but sensibly gave it considerable autonomy, and the Garhwal has continued as an intriguingly different part of India ever since.

Hinduism and its caste rules were far more relaxed there than down on the plain; Brahmin priests ate meat, while *dalits* (the 'oppressed' or so-called 'untouchables') led a more communal life with their neighbours.

More recently that independent spirit had been put to the test. After Independence, the Garhwal was subsumed into Uttar Pradesh, a vast province mainly in the plains, the Texas of India, as part of which it had struggled to be heard. Eventually the Garhwalis successfully agitated for their own separate state, to be called Uttaranchal, which was inaugurated the very month we were there.

Nor had it been easy financially. The Bhotia people had traditionally earned their living by trading with Tibet over the nearby passes. They were Tibetan in origin and had kept many of their habits, often counting in Tibetan to five and only thereafter in Urdu. Buddhist prayer-flags often flew from their Hindu temples. But after the disastrous Indo-China War of 1962, the border had been closed and they had turned more to agriculture, for which they needed the now forbidden high pastures around Nanda Devi. It was not surprising that poaching musk deer or supplementing subsistence crops with marijuana were becoming increasingly attractive options.

Bishen, a Bhotia, mentioned that he had family living in the village – and that his sister had married Gaura Devi's brother. I pricked up my ears. Gaura Devi was a legendary figure of whom I had heard much when travelling in the area before, but I had never realised that she had been born in Lata, in the shadow of Nanda Devi.

Bishen suggested that we go to see his brother-in-law, Devendra, and soon we were drinking tea on a flat tin roof looking out over the valley, as Devendra told me his sister's story.

Gaura Devi had been the public face of Chipko, the protest movement that had swept through the Indian Himalaya in the 1970s, attracting worldwide notice. This was due to the simplicity of its guiding idea: that to prevent forestry companies coming in to cut down their trees wholesale, each villager would hold onto a tree: *chipko* means 'hug'. As many of the leaders of the movement, like Gaura Devi, were female, this had instant international appeal in the seventies: an indigenous ecological movement seemingly run by women against uncaring multinationals.

The reality was both more complex and more interesting. A natural respect for the forests had always run deep in the Garhwali psyche, for both religious and practical reasons, long before the movement started. Giant deodars were often planted near their temples, and the idea of 'sacred groves' that could not be touched was common in the mountains. It was a long-held belief that if you felled a whole hillside of trees, landslides would inevitably follow.

In 1970 a ferocious monsoon had caused terrible floods and landslides down the Alakananda valley as far as Rishikesh. Bridges had been swept away, hundreds of houses had been destroyed and many people had been killed. This had touched off long-simmering grievances. The worst landslides had occurred downhill from where the forestry companies had been working. The result was the Chipko movement.

My friend Yatish Bahaguna, who'd been a Chipko activist at the time, had told me of the growing excitement in the valley as the villagers realised that they could resist the logging companies and stand up for their rights. In the teashops that form the heart of Garhwali village life, the young activists would tell of tactics that had worked elsewhere, with a strain of Gandhian thought thrown in. Their audience was largely female, as many of the men had been forced to take jobs down on the plain and send remittance money home; women traditionally gathered firewood in the forests, so they could see the depredations of the logging companies at first hand.

Things were brought to a head at the nearby village of Reni in 1974, where Gaura Devi was living. She was then in her late forties and had not had an easy life, having been widowed at twenty-two and left to bring up a son on her own. She had been involved in the Gandhian campaign for prohibition in the hills, to counter the alcoholism born from subsistence living and the despair of the remittance culture; this campaign had been largely driven by women. Gaura had become the head of the village Women's Club.

A forestry company had marked up thousands of trees for felling. Knowing that it would cause a violent reaction, they arranged for those able-bodied men who remained in the village to be called away to a town downriver, ostensibly to receive compensation for their losses after the 1962 war.

Then the contractors drove towards the village, parked some distance away and tried to skirt around the houses to reach the trees above. A young girl spotted them and warned Gaura Devi. Gaura mobilised the women and marched them up the hill. In the popular imagination, they are said to have held onto the trees and refused to let go, even after considerable threats of violence from the loggers. Whether they actually hugged the trees or not, they put up enough of a protest to make the loggers leave. The Hindu newspaper reported: 'One of the officials who was drunk brandished a gun. The women stood in a row, each one of them looking as if the mountain goddess Nanda Devi had taken one of her fiercest forms.'

The victory of an illiterate peasant woman over a large logging company was broadcast all over India. Gaura Devi became a heroine. Her own simple statement was: 'We have no quarrel with anyone but we only wanted to make the people understand that our existence is tied with the forests.'

Her Gandhian simplicity was echoed by a charismatic social worker, Sunderlal Bahaguna, who carried the Chipko movement onto the national stage. Bahaguna began to go on attention-grabbing hunger strikes and took his argument all the way to Indira Gandhi, then Prime Minister.

The government was forced to back down. An initial moratorium of ten years was put on all logging activities, and commercial logging has declined still further since.

It would be wonderful to report that the Chipko movement had spread all over India and met with similar success – but it did not. The Garhwal has a unique position, which it was able to exploit. The area is an emotive one, given that four great Hindu pilgrimage sites are near by and that the forests are considered to be the locks of Shiva, descending from the Himalaya to the Ganges. The nearest Western equivalent would be the English Lake District or Pikes Peak in the States. And while other areas of India were heartened by the Chipko ideal, they could not find quite the same determined communal stand that seemed to come naturally to the people of the mountains.

In the Garhwal, the movement continued and addressed other problems – in particular the decision by the government of Uttar Pradesh to build a dam at Tehri, flooding a vast area and displacing 100,000 people. The name of Gaura Devi was often invoked as a symbol of the people's pride.

But as for what had happened to Gaura Devi herself, I had heard nothing until now.

It was not a good story. She had died, according to her brother, in 'utter penury' some ten years before in 1991, aged sixty-six. As a sop to the idea of 'sustainable development', the women of her village had been trained to prepare potato chips and preserve fruit. However, there had been no training in how to sell their produce to the lowland towns and the project had ended in failure. The men of Lata, Reni and the surrounding villages were still forced to find work on the plains below.

What Gaura had apparently most wanted was for the Nanda Devi area to be accessible again. This was not just so

that Lata men could work as porters on the expeditions –
although this had been a lucrative, if occasional, source
of income. It was rather that without their traditional
high pasturage and access to the all-important traditional
medicines, like angelica, the rural economy was wilting.
The only alternatives were poaching musk deer or
growing cannabis. Her brother turned to me: 'Please rec-
ommend that this area is opened up again, so that our
young men can stay here and work, instead of having to
leave the village.'

*

Back at the camp below the village, I found an excited
John Shipton. Although it had been late afternoon when
we'd arrived, he had insisted on climbing up the small
Lata Peak nearby – small in comparison to the giants
around us, but still a healthy ascent of 4,500 feet with no
paths to guide him. Why? Because that is what his father
had done in 1934, running up in light tennis shoes with
Tilman to get an idea of their surroundings.

I was beginning to realise that when John described
Nanda Devi as 'the subconscious siren calling me all my
life', he wasn't kidding. What was also clear was the kick
he got whenever he did anything to emulate his father.
Now he was on a high, bubbling over with excitement.
He persuaded me to play *pisaru*, a Pakistani game he had
learnt in the Karakoram. The others were playing bridge,
but I sensed that John was not a natural bridge player. He
taught me the rules of *pisaru*, 'But you can forget all the
rules. Really the trick is just to throw your cards down

hard enough. It's all about *karma*. And if it starts going your way, everything will go your way.'

I remembered what Tilman had written of his friend's son, when John had accompanied him on one of his ocean voyages: 'Like his father, John loved talking and arguments, but had such volubility, such a rush of words to the mouth, that when I was concerned I had to have everything repeated in slow time before I got the message.'

'I've never had a real job,' said John, apropos of nothing, as we played. 'I've bummed around. Crewing for ships around the world, teaching English, travelling. I'm going to be fifty soon. In fact my birthday's around the day we should be entering the Sanctuary. If we do. If we get up this bloody gorge. It's excitingly terrifying, isn't it?'

Our campsite at Lata was set in a crescent between the village and the Dhaoli Ganges. I left the others playing cards in their tents and sat by the water, in the evening sun, listening to a tape that a friend had made for me before I left. As the sun shone low from the west, it started raining overhead and I lay back in the heat, letting the cold rain fall on my naked chest, a terrific feeling as I looked north up the river valley towards Mount Kamet and Tibet.

A rainbow appeared, neatly spanning the river and almost too neatly signifying what lay beyond – the long climb up to the Sanctuary. The wind whipped grains of Gangetic sand across the sun, the mica flashing like grains of gold. I experienced an intense epiphany of complete happiness – heightened by the knowledge that the next few days were going to be hell.

*

We set off the next day with an uneven straggle of local porters accompanying us. To Akshay's alarm, some of them had asked if they could follow on later, as there was a wedding in the village. I shared his foreboding, as I liked to feel that my tent was ahead, not behind me.

When Shipton and Tilman had come here, they had worked with three groups of helpers, who had not always got on with each other: the Sherpas, who were effectively mountaineering co-members of the team and shared everything with the two Englishmen, to the extent that Shipton prophetically described them as 'the only way for us ever to climb Everest'; some experienced Nepalese porters; and some local Bhotia porters, from Lata and Mana, to make up the numbers. As might have been expected by anybody except Shipton and Tilman, who were not always good on human relations, the attempt to mix Nepalese and local porters was unsuccessful, and there were fierce arguments. At one point 'the more hot-tempered on both sides were shouting and grimacing and threatening each other with fists and sticks' and Tilman had to separate them physically.

One little-reported reason for bringing Sherpas all the way from Nepal, despite the considerable complications (Shipton expends a whole chapter in his book on their travel arrangements), was that Sherpas were free of the caste rules that meant that both Nepalese and Bhotia porters could not share food with their British employers; as Shipton pointed out, 'on a long and difficult task, this would impose an impossible situation.'

Just as we left the village, we came to the small local temple. The white plaster walls were covered with paintings of Nanda Devi – not as a peak but as a Hindu goddess, for the mountain is worshipped throughout Garhwal as Parvati, the consort of Shiva, in her younger, bridal form: the word 'devi' means goddess. In a few weeks' time a great annual *jat* (a pilgrimage) was to be made here from across the region.

The goddess Nanda Devi has a particular resonance for the women of the Garhwal, for she is, like many of them, a *dhiyani* or 'bride who has left her village'. According to Hindu theology, she has departed from her own mountain to live with her husband Shiva in his remote abode on Mount Kailash in Tibet. Many of the women in the Garhwal suffer considerably from just such distant marriages, living far from home with unsympathetic in-laws, and the female suicide-rate is considerably higher than it is for men.

Once a year, the goddess Nanda Devi, like all such brides, is allowed to return to her place of birth by the mountain, and it is this annual home-coming which the pilgrims celebrate.

We were waylaid by a very old man just inside the temple compound. He looked battered by life; his glasses were tied on with string and he wore a military-looking overcoat that had seen better days. This Ancient Mariner figure introduced himself as Dewan Singh Butola. He was ninety-five. To my astonishment, it emerged that he had been one of the porters on the very first expedition to summit Nanda Devi in 1936, and he remembered Tilman and the other 'sahibs' well: 'He [Tilman] loved the porters – he gave us a kilo of rice every day and lots of tea, sugar and *ata*. He paid us three rupees a day.'

John Shipton, Steve Berry and I stayed for a while to listen to Dewan Singh, as he reminisced in front of one of the images of Nanda Devi. Dewan recalled an incident by the Deodi bridge, of which Tilman had also left an account: the Nepalese porters had turned back, but the local Bhotias like Dewan had carried on, with the result that both the Bhotias and the 'sahibs' had had to carry double loads. Dewan returned to this point several times. It was clearly a matter of some pride – and, as Tilman had also pointed out, if the Bhotias had followed the Nepalese and 'deserted', the ascent would have been impossible.

Dewan Singh's bitterest memory was of the Indian Liaison Officer with them; then, as now, such an official had to accompany the expedition: 'He kept the clothes that the Sahib [Tilman] had ordered for us and pretended they had never arrived. So we never had any warm clothes. And the Liaison Officer kept them.' He didn't need to add, 'The bastard,' but his face said it all. The coat Dewan was now wearing also looked like a relic from a past expedition, for he had been on many since.

He had also been with the French when they attempted their fatal traverse between Nanda Devi's twin peaks in 1951; the two lead summiteers had died. Dewan Singh said that the French had treated the early part of the expedition as an extended hunting trip, shooting many *bharal* and birds; it was hardly surprising that Nanda Devi (he gestured at her picture on the temple walls) had not taken kindly to them.

Some of the porters made offerings at the temple before leaving for the Sanctuary, which, given their youth, almost none of them had seen before. Dewan watched us all go, his eyes almost invisible behind the thick pebbles of his glasses.

We could not have had a more beautiful morning to leave Lata. The villagers were gathering the October harvest in fields ringed by marigolds and dark red amaranthus, 'love-lies-bleeding', grown as a decorative cottage garden plant back in England but for its oil here. Back-lit by the sun, the amaranthus glowed with particular intensity and I remembered Milton's lines:

> Immortal Amarant, a Flower which once
> In Paradise, fast by the Tree of Life
> Began to bloom . . .

I had brought a copy of *Paradise Lost* with me, or at least a manageable section of it: Book Four, which included Satan's guided tour of the prelapsarian Garden of Eden. As we climbed above Lata village and into the woods I thought of the 'Groves whose rich Trees wept odorous Gumms and Balme'. Indeed, the reason I had brought the book was that I suspected that Milton had travelled here long before me.

As Satan first approaches the borders of Eden, he passes through thick forests of cedar, pine and fir, which lie beneath the high plateau of Paradise, surrounded by its high wall. The approach to that 'steep, savage hill' seems impenetrable to man or beast, 'so thick entwined as one continued brake' is the undergrowth. Satan leaps over these defences and surveys the whole of Paradise from the highest tree, the Tree of Life. The topography that follows is very precise, as Milton describes the landscape, for this is not the flat Garden of Eden that we are used to from pictorial representations; there is a great mountain at its centre and from this mountain, 'with many a rill', a river flows out and 'murmuring waters fall down the steep slopes, dispersed'.

The river that issues from Paradise is a central image of Milton's Eden; he goes to considerable trouble to describe its progress and how it irrigates the whole plateau ('Southward through Eden went a river large'). He follows Genesis in describing it as dividing into four further rivers after leaving Paradise. The first of these rivers, 'Pison', was commonly identified by authorities such as St Jerome, St Ambrose and St Epiphanus as being the Ganges itself.

Perhaps this is why the mythical source of the Ganges gets a surprising amount of attention from Milton, given that the true geographical source was not to be discovered for another two centuries. At one point he compares Satan to a vulture who flies down from the north over China towards 'the Springs of Ganges', and later he soars over the river when looking for the animal best suited to seducing Eve.

Milton's Paradise is a composite drawn from many sources, both classical and literary, and he lists many of them in the poem. Aside from Genesis, Milton draws on elements from *Arabia Felix* and Greek mythology. But his final and most resonant comparison was the one that interested me most: he compares the walled garden to 'Mount Amara', the mythical retreat of Abyssinian kings,

> by some supposed
> True Paradise under the Ethiop Line
> By Nilus' head, enclosed with shining rock
> A whole day's journey high . . .

Mount Amara was an idea that had a fascination for Milton and his contemporaries, from one of whom, Peter Heylyn, the author of a *Cosmographie in Four Bookes* (1652), Milton had borrowed the description that it was 'a dayes journey high: the Rock so smooth and even . . . that no wall can be more evenly polished'. Heylyn describes the actual peak as being surrounded by a high wall, with gardens within that wall. It had 'such ravishing pleasures of all sorts, that some have taken (but mistaken) it for the place of *Paradise*'. Moreover Mount Amara was thought to be on the equator, so that it would enjoy eternal spring.

The image of a remote, inaccessible mountain sanctuary like Amara, which is the source of a river, had already enjoyed wide currency since Mandeville's wild tales of Prester John in the fourteenth century. In the century following Milton, it became a staple literary archetype of pastoral convention.

By the time of Samuel Johnson, it was such a familiar setting that he could appropriate it for his moral fable *Rasselas* as 'Amhara', the 'happy valley', in which his princes live a secluded life of luxury: 'the kingdom of Amhara, surrounded on every side by mountains, of which the summits overhang the middle part'.

In the nineteenth century, it becomes the 'Mount Abora', which Coleridge's 'damsel with a dulcimer' sings of in *Kubla Khan*, and the whole of that poem is a meditation on a secluded sanctuary 'girdled round' with walls and towers. Samuel Butler again uses the same idea of a mountain sanctuary, which he calls 'Erewhon' (an anagram of 'nowhere') for his satire of 1857, a previously undiscovered country, which the narrator only reaches after crossing a range of difficult peaks.

For the Victorian explorers who first saw them at around this time, the Himalaya were a perfect backdrop on which to project such literary landscapes as they stumbled into this new dreamland. They had been used to the Alps, a small concentrated group of mountains up to 15,000 feet high. Now they were confronted by a mountain range longer than the whole of Europe, with peaks over 25,000 feet. It was as if they had left a solar system and found a galaxy.

No wonder their imaginations ran riot. This was a generation whose adventures in mountaineering had often started in the Lake District, both physically and metaphorically, prompted by Wordsworth's and Coleridge's quest for the sublime. Their new 'abode of snow' geomorphed before them into a rich landscape of interpretation that mixed local legends, like the Buddhist notion of Shambhala or 'Shangri-La' as it became known in the West, with their own cultural inheritance.

It is hardly surprising that the early Victorian travellers should have been so excited that one of the sources of the Ganges did indeed have an 'Eden-like seclusion', was ringed with a wall of mountains and was also inaccessible. Literature had prefigured geography in the most remarkable way. The quest to enter the sanctuary was as much fuelled by the literary imagination as by geographical necessity.

But there was one constant to all these fictional precursors of Nanda Devi: the sanctuary, once discovered, was corrupted, or in some way found to be imperfect. Satan destroys Eden for Adam and Eve, who leave 'hand in hand with wandering steps and slow'. Prince Rasselas likewise departs the mountain refuge of 'Amhara', dissatisfied with a life of such perfect ease. And even in Xanadu, Kubla Khan hears 'ancestral voices prophesying war'.

Implicit in the idea of entering a sanctuary was the idea of its fall.

*

The forests above Lata were magnificent. Autumn was beginning to set the yellow of the mixed birches and pines against the red of the berberis, and there was a white carpet of 'pearly everlasting' over the ground. Rock roses tumbled over the path, and the wild thyme gave off a strong smell as foot after foot brushed against it. There were potentilla and campanula, familiar sights in the average garden, but more unbuttoned here, as well as rare anemones and alliums.

I have never understood why the most famous area of

the Himalaya is Tibet, with its arid, endless plateau in the northern rain-shadow of the mountains, when the more beautiful southern side in India and Bhutan, with its spectacular, dense forest – once memorably described by Robert Byron as 'an inverted arboretum' – should be so ignored.

John Shipton was in seventh heaven. Back in Wales he ran a bulb nursery – 'It's our busiest time of year, I should really be there now helping Alison with the orders,' he would occasionally murmur, in a not very heartfelt way – and he was continually on his knees with a Himalayan flora book. Wearing a yellow turban, John looked like an eccentric Victorian plant gatherer as he carefully collected seeds from unusual anemones. Given the chance, he would have stayed for hours, had it not been too late in the year for many species to be still seeding.

I was feeling pretty good myself. I had that 'Day One' freshness to my boots and clothes, the sun was shining with a perfect light for photography, Bishen was chatting to me idly as we took pictures and a white wagtail had decided to accompany me up the forest glades. The fact that there was a 5,000-foot climb ahead was a mild deterrent but it would doubtless pass easily.

Then I heard a voice thundering behind me: 'This is fucking ridiculous. Where are those bloody porters?' Mac was back. He strode up the path to join me and carried on the conversation from where we had left off a few nights before. He was still concerned whether we were all going to make it to the top of the Sanctuary – and what he was going to write for his report.

He used me as a sounding board. I had never been involved in the politics of mountaineering before, nor had I much wanted to be. But Mac, as the President of the International Mountaineering and Climbing Federation, was at its centre.

His stance was simple. Mountains were there to be climbed; however, just as when boys want to steal apples, there always seemed to be a farmer trying to stop mountaineers from doing so.

For years before the Second World War, the whole of Nepal had been closed to British climbers – one reason for Nanda Devi being such a lure. Even when the Nepalese finally opened up their route to Everest, the Chinese promptly closed the approach from the other side. And there were many restrictions still in place elsewhere – as Mac commented with particular vehemence, there were always 'problems with fucking religion'. No one had been able to climb Kangchenjunga in Sikkim for some time, while many Bhutanese peaks remained off limits. Indeed, the highest remaining unclimbed mountains in the world were all in Bhutan, where rigidly orthodox Buddhist sentiment held that it would be a transgression to set foot on them.

Meanwhile other more accessible mountains were getting over-crowded. There were tales of people fighting each other on the Matterhorn to get onto fixed-rope sections, of peak-time traffic on Mont Blanc and of queues forming to use the ice ladders on Everest.

But the simple answer to this – to open the 'closed' peaks like Nanda Devi – was not so easy. The example of

Everest, with its detritus and unburied dead, loomed large. Mountaineering had become a dirty business, and trekking was often no better. The deforestation of areas of Nepal by porters who burnt local wood rather than carry fuel had become a byword. Who would wish that on the beautiful untouched forest around us?

The example of Bhutan offered a possible way forward. The smallest of the Himalayan countries had adopted the much-applauded approach of letting in only a few high-paying trekkers, for minimum impact on the landscape and maximum benefit to the local economy. Perhaps, mused Mac, some similar scheme could work for Nanda Devi, with licensed porters bringing in their own fuel under super-vision by Government Liaison Officers, and expeditions paying an 'ecology levy' to support this. But as Dewan Singh's story back in the village had illustrated, this would be open to abuse by Liaison Officers and officials.

We came to a clearing and found 'Bull' Kumar pausing for a rest. He was finding the going tough, which was not surprising given his age. And, as Mac whispered to me in an aside that could have been heard back in Joshimath, Bull had lost all his toes on a previous expedition. He was using a stick and had a young lad with him as a guide, but it was clear that nothing was going to stop him. I have rarely met a man of such adamantine will.

This was the first time I'd had a chance to talk to him properly, as in the days leading up to the expedition he had been engulfed in a flurry of last-minute negotiations with the mountaineering authorities. But I knew him well by reputation.

Bull was the Chris Bonington of India, in terms of public profile and the amount of climbs he had led, and, like Bonington, he had left some good accounts of them. Bull would be the first to claim that he was not a great literary stylist – in one book he says: 'Writing is not my line and if I had my way I would rather climb the peak again than write about it' – but his plain prose style told some remarkable stories that were almost completely unknown in the West.

For twenty years between 1960 and 1981, he had led a series of expeditions that were sometimes controversial but undeniably brave, particularly as the equipment available to the Indian climbers was often painfully inadequate compared to that used by Western mountaineers. No possum fur lined their boots.

Bull was also the one member of the party who had already been to the Sanctuary, although he had not taken this particular route before. As we wandered through the woods, Mac fell unusually silent and respectful as we listened to Bull's tales.

In the early 1960s, the Indians had only been allowed access to Everest intermittently (1960, 1962, 1965), so in the 'off' years between they had attempted some of the major peaks in the Garhwal.

In 1961, having got to within 200 yards of the summit of Everest the year before, Bull was determined to make a successful ascent of Nilakantha, the 'blue-throated one', a ferocious and beautiful peak north of Joshimath. He described it to us as 'almost my Waterloo'. They had left late in the spring and so were racing the monsoon, with thin boots and little survival gear. Nilakantha is 21,600 feet high, lower than Nanda Devi but a formidable technical climb. As Bull confessed, in his beautifully modulated Indian accent, 'I had a sense of fear and awe whenever I thought of Nilakantha.'

And for Bull, this was not just another peak as it would have been for a European expedition; this was in the Hindu heartland that Shankara had created around Garhwal, a peak with tremendous symbolic resonance. As they set off for the mountain, the cries of pilgrims echoed after them: '*Jai Badri Vishal!* Hail to the Lord of Badrinath!'

Bull and his team were stuck in an ice gully for three days, with no food and nothing but snow to eat. His account of this was, as ever, graphic: 'We were in bad shape. Sharma's lips had turned septic and pus was oozing out of them, like a monstrous gargoyle spouting putrescent blood.' As they had inadequate boots, they could only wait for frostbite to take its toll. This was when Bull had lost his toes.

But they were still determined to reach the summit. Bull had a wonderful description of the mood that came over them as they waited: 'We had become *detached* – the sort of detachment that a high altitude pilot experiences, or that saints and sages experience when they retire into their mountain fastnesses.'

When the weather calmed, he sent his best men off towards the top. They came back and said they had summited. However, at the ensuing press conference there was considerable controversy when the claims of the lead climbers seemed to contradict one another. At one point Bull shouted at them to shut up.

I knew that there had always been a schism in Indian mountaineering between the high-profile military teams and the ordinary civilian climbers, who naturally resented the preferential access to peaks that the military expeditions were given. The civilians controlled the *Himalayan Journal* and were centred in Bombay. They seized on the confusion of this incident, which became the start of a bitter and long-running battle between the two camps, with the civilians claiming that the military expeditions were a little too eager to claim peaks at all costs. Even thirty years later, their account of Bull's Nilakantha expedition still referred to 'great controversy, not settled, despite acceptance of the claim by an investigating committee'. Bull reacted to this controversy with characteristic bravado; he bluntly titled his book *Nilakantha: The First Ascent*.

Bull spent nearly a year in hospital after Nilakantha. Meanwhile the Indians had another crack at Everest — this time getting even closer to the top, but still 400 feet short.

In 1964 there was talk of an expedition to Nanda Devi. Officially, it had not been climbed successfully since Tilman's 1936 expedition; the lead climbers of the 1951 French team disappeared in their attempt, and they were still below the summit when they were last seen.

Originally the Indian attempt was to have been led by another military climber, Gurdial Singh, but when he saw the poor state of the equipment he refused. So Bull was appointed instead, to the initial dismay of the team, who complained, according to Bull and much to Mac's amusement, 'that they were being led by a man without any toes'.

Bull proved his leadership qualifications immediately. He remembered that after the recent Indo-China War of 1962, American Special Forces had been in the area and had left plentiful supplies of the best mountain equipment in storage: 'Proper down sleeping bags, parkas, wonderful boots,' said Bull, his voice still sounding like that of a small boy at Christmas all these years later. Bull managed to commandeer them for the expedition, although he was asked to indemnify them personally by a government minister, the powerful H.C. Sarin. Chancing his luck – and initially as a joke – Bull asked Sarin if he could have a helicopter as well, an unheard-of luxury. The minister agreed. After all the failures on Everest, the Indian Government was desperate to have a mountaineering success.

So Bull was able to fly supplies into the Sanctuary, a hair-raising task as helicopters react erratically to the strong thermals and cross-winds of the Himalaya. He flew in with the helicopter himself and later wrote: 'Once above the Rishi Gorge I saw what is perhaps the world's most magnificent snow panorama, a veritable dreamland.' Bull could recognise the phalanx of immense mountains that ringed Nanda Devi and guarded the approaches to the Sanctuary: Dunagiri; 'the formidable yellow and black spire of Changabang, still unclimbed, and no wonder'; and a roll-call of other big peaks: 'Berthali, Msigthuni and Devistan, all glistening in the morning sun. And then all of a sudden, immediately before us, stood the most majestic of all, the Ushba of the Himalaya, the Blessed Goddess, Nanda Devi.'

Bull went up with his team to Camp III at 21,200 feet. From there they launched a summit attempt. It was successful. To make absolutely sure that his enemies could not carp at this, Bull got the lead climbers to leave an Indian tricolour flag on the top, which was photographed from a plane a few days later.

There was a tremendous explosion of national emotion all over India at this achievement. The greatest mountain in the country – and a Hindu goddess – had been climbed by a wholly Indian team.

Bull was a hero. He stopped Mac and me in a little glade that we had reached and looked back over the valley towards Lata, which was now some way below. 'They gave me every medal they had. I became the most decorated man in India!' he said with a laugh. 'People spend their entire lives wanting just one of the little medals I wear on the third row down.'

The success on Nanda Devi reinvigorated Indian climbing. The next year yet another Indian expedition attempted Everest, led by Captain Mohan S. Kohli and with Bull as deputy leader. This time they not only succeeded but placed four different teams on the summit over a ten-day period, a formidable achievement.

Bull went on to lead many other expeditions. But there had been tragedies. A later expedition to Everest in 1985 led by his brother, Kiran Kumar, had ended with the death of Kiran and five others, including some who had been with Bull on Nanda Devi. One of Bull's own sons had died in a separate mountaineering accident.

In many ways, the ascent of Nanda Devi had been Bull's greatest success. Although it was some twenty years since he had led his last official expedition, he had remained active and now wanted to go on this very last journey back to Nanda Devi, 'before I hang up my boots'.

The determination with which he had managed to persuade the Indian Government to let him do so was awe-inspiring: 'First I went to the Environment Ministry. They said that Uttar Pradesh had jurisdiction over Nanda Devi as a state. So I went to the Uttar Pradesh state legislature, but they sent me back to Central Government. Because of the involvement of foreigners, I was referred to the Home Ministry, who brought in the Defence Ministry and the External Affairs Ministry. And of course I needed Indian Mountaineering Federation involvement as well.'

From my relatively simple involvement with Indian bureaucrats when obtaining film permits, I knew all too well what this meant in terms of time lost through procrastination. The ability to climb up through government agencies is something that the great leaders of mountaineering expeditions – Bonington, Dyhrenfurth or Bull himself – have needed quite as much as any skills on the mountains themselves.

*

We had climbed some 4,000 feet from the village and the lush vegetation of the forest was petering out. By the time we reached the top and the little meadow called Lata

Kharak, there was nothing but scrubby rhododendrons and azaleas.

Lata Kharak was on a beautiful but exposed ridge at 12,500 feet, with sweeping views east to the magnificent dome of Trisul. 'That was my first big summit,' said Bull coming up behind me and looking over towards it. 'I was sent there by Tenzing [Norgay, of Everest 1953 fame] when I was just a young lieutenant. I was going to ask the authorities for half a *lakh* to pay for the expedition, but Tenzing told me that no one would take me seriously unless I asked for at least a whole *lakh* – so I did, and I got it. Great man, Tenzing.'

It was Tenzing who, encouraged by Nehru, had set up the Himalayan Mountaineering Institute in Darjeeling where Bull had trained, part of an attempt by Nehru to create a generation of Indian climbers who could compete on the world stage.

Mac later told me that Bull had not only climbed Trisul but was famous for having skied back down it. 'And that took a lot of balls,' said Mac.

From Lata Kharak we could also see the beginnings of the Rishi Ganges gorge as it ran towards the Nanda Devi massif, a great widening crack that seemed to have been chiselled through the mountains, pushing such towering peaks as Bethartholi Himal, Nanda Ghunti and Hathi Parbat off to the side. The gorge already looked terrifying from above. I couldn't help thinking how much worse it would be when we were at its foot and looking up at its head, the only way into the Inner Sanctuary.

It was lucky that Lata Kharak had such a compelling

view, as we had plenty of time to take it in. The porters had still not arrived with the tents. Akshay Kumar was looking worried. He was acutely conscious that this was an expedition sanctioned not only by the International Mountaineering and Climbing Federation but by his own father. 'It appears the porters have celebrated at the wedding a little too much,' he announced, as various inebriated Lata men made their way unsteadily over the hill. It was long past nightfall before everyone's tent and baggage had arrived. Having foreseen this, I had packed a few Absolut Vodka miniatures in my rucksack, along with a down jacket, but it was a relief when the cook, Sula, arrived and dished up a large chilli soup.

That night the talk was all of past expeditions and summits climbed – stories of the Karakoram, of Nanga Parbat, of the Mountains of the Moon and of the Red Peak in Russia. George Band and Mac were the veterans at this; with a cumulative hundred years of mountaineering between them, they could give us a virtual reality tour of seemingly every peak on the planet. George had an encyclopaedic memory, Mac an acute eye for the specific detail or anecdote, but even between them they would sometimes forget: 'Now what *was* the name of that German climber lost on K2 that year?' They would throw it open to the group, and then continue.

I listened as they wove stories out of the legends: what was it exactly, on the first ascent of Annapurna, that Herzog had said to his social inferior Lachenal to annoy him so, before the nightmarish, frost-bitten descent when Herzog lost his gloves? What had Heinrich Harrer (the controversial author of *Seven Years in Tibet*, accused of Nazi sympathies) told George about Harrer's own failure to climb Kangchenjunga? How Hunt, proved medically unfit ten years before to lead an expedition, had managed to pass his test for the 1953 Everest trip: the Queen's doctor examining them all had said that what mattered was not fitness but 'spirit' and had simply measured their height.

According to Mac, Russian mountaineers of the Stalinist era were supposed to abstain from sex for six months before attempting a peak. Mac and a companion had shared a campsite with a party of them on some nameless range in the Caucasus. As Mac spoke no Russian and they didn't speak English, communication had been limited. At one point Mac had asked them if, given the abstinence order, they masturbated a lot, and had made a graphic gesture to illustrate his point. The Russians had misunderstood this as a proposition from Mac. From then on, they insisted that the British team sleep well away from their own tent.

Everyone laughed at this. Well, almost everyone. Bull seemed to have fallen asleep, rocking slightly over a large tumbler of whisky that Mac had been distributing. Then, a full minute after everyone else, he gave a deep rumbling chuckle, like the distant roar of an avalanche falling towards a glacier: 'Bloody Russians!'

*

Two rings of mountains radiate out from Nanda Devi, forming an inner and outer 'curtain' to the Sanctuary.

We now had to climb over the outer curtain. As Shipton and Tilman had found, the only way to do this was to get over the Dharansi pass, on the shoulders of Mount Dunagiri.

This had caused problems for many expeditions: Bull had nearly lost a porter, who had fallen 300 feet but had miraculously survived; an earlier Indian expedition in 1961 had been forced back by an avalanche and had then spent four days trying to get over the pass. W.H. Murray had struggled over it in 1950 ('I cannot recall ever having felt so exhausted before') and was only revived when he discovered some old sweets in his pocket, which a friend had given him on leaving Glasgow. I was impressed by another Scotsman, W.W. Graham, for pioneering the route in the first place in 1883. There was no natural logic to the way it draped across the folds of Dunagiri, disappearing up and down gullies.

Shipton and his porters had not found it easy either, crossing in spring when there was still some snow on the ground. Shipton said his heart was in his mouth as he watched the porters carrying their loads along the narrow ridges of this section. He and Tilman had problems in even finding the pass, as it was not clearly visible from below. They spotted three small notches on the skyline and tried each one. By the time they discovered that, in the usual way, only the last one was navigable, night had fallen. They bivouacked high on the pass for the night.

As always, such hardships brought out the best in Shipton: 'As I lay on my little platform ... I was filled with a deep content, untroubled either by the memory of the failures of the day, or by the prospect of further trials on the morrow.'

We had no snow, but as George Band laconically commented, 'there was a surprising amount of exposure' on the exacting climb up there, with a long traverse around the side. At 14,000 feet, this was the first real test of everyone's fitness at altitude.

As we climbed, we saw Himalayan griffin vultures flying over us, and further above there were lammergeyers with their impossibly wide wingspans, circling in the way I was used to seeing condors in the Andes.

A bad moment came when, as I happily settled into a traverse, thinking that the climbing was over, the porters ahead of me suddenly ascended what appeared to be a vertical gully. However, after a final scramble up the same 'boulder-strewn slope' that Shipton had taken, I could look down on the hanging valley of Dharansi beyond.

Originally we had planned to stay there, but there was a problem with the water supply. Instead we were trying, ambitiously, to do two days' journey in one and press on to the next campsite at the meadow of Dibrugheta below. In retrospect this was perhaps pushing too far. I was beginning to feel the strain of the altitude, the sun and the distance by the time we reached Dharansi, and others in the group were behind me.

There were the broken-down remains of a small shed on the Dharansi plateau, from the days when Lata men were allowed access here for the grazing. It provided the only available shade and I found two of our party, Jeff Ford and Barry Bond, taking shelter there. These two had

trekked together before and, although professing themselves overawed by the mountaineering company they
were now keeping, were a welcome source of occasionally
raucous humour whenever the group started to take themselves too seriously. They were from the Midlands; Jeff
worked in biotechnology, while Barry was in the water
industry. I had first noticed them on the plane when they
had asked the Swedish air hostess if she had a banana: 'I
am not sure I understand you absolutely. Why is it you
want a banana?'

Now Barry was in a bad way. His skin had gone grey
and he was sucking constantly at a catheter tube he had
rigged up from the bottle in his knapsack to his mouth.
We looked down at the considerable 3,000-foot slope
dropping away below us, filled with scree. 'Well, it could
be worse,' said Jeff, who subscribed wholeheartedly to
the glass half full approach, 'we could be at the bottom,
climbing up. Better get on with it then.'

We talked as much as we could to keep Barry going.
This proved easy as Jeff had an unexpected obsession: he
collected signed first-edition mountaineering books, but
was unusual in that he tried to get the signatures not only
of the author but of all those who had taken part in that
expedition. This meant a marathon of cross-referencing
to get a completely signed 'association copy'. One of the
things he was most enjoying about the trip was getting so
many books autographed by the cumulative talent. Bull's
signature alone was apparently worth the journey.

By the time Jeff had finished describing his collection
in detail, we had lost considerable altitude and Barry had

regained his colour. The harsh scree slopes softened out and we came down through a forest filled with birches and tree-ferns lit up by the late afternoon light. We could hear the streams leading into the Rishi Ganges long before we saw them.

Then we came to the beautiful meadow of Dibrugheta. I could immediately see why Shipton and Tilman had fallen on it with such relief, as 'a horizontal oasis in a vertical desert'. When they had seen it, in spring, it would have been carpeted by iris, white garlic and forget-me-nots. Even in late summer, the meadow was still full of tall angelica, roses, cotoneaster and Himalayan asters, with ranks of *Abies spectabilis*, the Himalayan fir, behind. Gentians scrambled in the little rock ledges around the meadow.

In the middle of Dibrugheta was a large white boulder that shone from a distance and had been a beacon to us, as it was our final destination for the night. It was big enough for a dozen men to lie on – we knew this, because we had seen some of the advance guard of porters doing just that as we descended towards them. Now we joined them. We were some of the first to arrive, along with Steve Berry. Then George came in, with his steady, relentless pace. But many of the others were strung out way behind us on the mountain and some were finding the going tough. Altitude had taken its toll.

Now, while we lay exhausted on the boulder in the middle of Dibrugheta meadow, the night came down and we knew that our companions were somewhere above and behind us on the cold plateau of Dharansi. We were cold ourselves. This was all virgin territory for many of the porters who had unceremoniously dumped loads all over the mountainside, unsure where we were stopping. As on the previous evening, we had no food or warm clothing.

Steve Berry collected as many of our head-torches as he could and together with Deva, the lead guide, headed back up the 3,000-foot slope to Dharansi to help the others. It was the equivalent of climbing Snowdon in the dark.

George Band and I lay on the large white rock that gleamed in the moonlight, trying to identify the constellations above us in what was a completely clear night sky, devoid of any light pollution. Then we saw flashes of light as Steve, Deva and their head-torches advanced up the steep face opposite. After a while, answering flashes of light started to descend towards them; the porters had stripped bark from the birches as they passed and lit them, for a peculiar and useful quality of the Himalayan birch, *Betula utilis*, is that it burns when green. When one fresh handful of birch had burnt out, the porters would peel a strip from another as they passed without even stopping and use the burning stump of the old torch to light the new.

During the long hours that we waited, as we watched the flickering lights bringing in the last of our companions and the tents, George told me of some of his early experiences after Everest. For the 1953 expedition had not been the high point of George's life, in either the metaphorical or the literal sense. On Everest he had waited below for Hillary and Tenzing to return. Two years later, in 1955, he was to summit himself on Kangchenjunga, an achievement that many mountaineers, including John Hunt, thought more considerable than Everest.

When Hunt and the others had gone out to Everest in 1953, Kangchenjunga (or 'Kange' as they referred to it among themselves) was their fall-back if things went wrong – and when, after the successful ascent, Hunt was asked what lay next, he unhesitatingly replied, 'Kangchenjunga.'

At 28,169 feet, Kangchenjunga was the third-highest mountain in the world. Until 1852 it had been thought to be the highest and it was certainly the most visible. Unlike Everest and K2, buried in the High Himalaya, it could be seen clearly from Darjeeling, and many a Victorian tea-planter had saluted it over their evening sundowner.

As well as being one of the highest, Kangchenjunga was also one of the world's largest mountains; the name means 'Five Treasures of the Snow', because it is not one peak but five, all over 8,000 metres. The massif covers so vast an area that few have ever circumnavigated it. 'The Five Treasures of the Snow' presented a daunting challenge.

The team who went there in 1955 was led by Charles Evans, a brilliant organiser who had been deputy leader on Everest, and it included many of that earlier party. As an added rogue element, they also took Joe Brown.

Joe Brown was straight out of Manchester, twenty-six, with a rockabilly quiff. He was part of the brash young rock-climbing school that had learnt their skills on the old mine shafts of Alderley Edge and the gritstone quarries of the Peak District; Mac had been another member of this running pack. Brown was untested at high altitude but was a potentially formidable mountaineer.

Brown's inclusion was a significant one. No one much liked to talk about climbing and class – it was supposed to be something that got left at ground-level, in the democracy of the mountains where, in Brown's own words, 'the fact that one person might be a professor and another a labourer had no relevance' – but inevitably, like most British activities, it seeped through in the end, particularly in the initial selection of climbers.

Previous Himalayan expeditions had been officer-caste, and in the 1950s the Alpine Club was a formidably stuffy institution. The way that George had been selected for the 1953 expedition was typical. Need a few more climbers? Apply to the Oxford and Cambridge clubs. The same principle had been in operation ever since Mallory had picked out the young Sandy Irvine from Oxford University for their fatal 1924 attempt on Everest.

This had ignored the considerable climbing talent of grass-roots, working-class areas bordering the Peak District and Merseyside, men who had climbed at weekends in associations such as the Gritstone Club and the Rock and Ice.

Joe Brown was typical of such clubs – a jobbing builder who biked down to the crags of North Wales from Manchester. Another was Don Whillans, although he was still considered 'too awkward a customer' to include in the trip to Kangchenjunga. But Whillans and other climbers were to lead the succeeding wave of British Himalayan climbing in the next few decades, the Bonington years, when rock-climbing skills learnt in Snowdonia were played out on the great faces of peaks over 26,000 feet.

Brown's inclusion in the 1955 Kangchenjunga expedition was the first break in the dyke – and, was made possible because it was officially only a 'reconnaissance expedition', so less pressurised than an official summit attempt.

When the telegram came asking him to join the expedition, Brown had so little money that he was forced to auction some of his climbing gear to pay for the ticket. On joining the others in the Himalaya, he was amazed that when they got into camp at the end of each day, the Sherpas would, in good batman fashion, 'have laid out your personal effects in a tidy order, inflated the lilo and unrolled your sleeping bag. You sat down in the tent and they pulled off your dirty boots and socks, replacing them with clean ones.'

Kangchenjunga lies between the borders of Nepal, Tibet and Sikkim, and this has always complicated the access to it. Earlier expeditions had probed the western, Nepalese approaches to the mountain, including one as early as 1905 led by Aleister Crowley, who had achieved notoriety as a black magician, the so-called 'Great Beast'; this was the approach route that Evans' group now took. George told me they had come across one of Crowley's abandoned camps above the Yalung glacier and found old champagne corks littered around it; the 'Great Beast' had liked to live well, although his expedition had ended in tragedy.

One of Crowley's companions, Alexis Pache, and three

porters had been caught in an avalanche and died. This was hardly uncommon, then or now. But what had shocked the world was Crowley's indifference to it. A newspaper quoted him as saying that he was 'not over-anxious in the circumstances . . . to render help. A mountain accident of this sort is one of the things for which I have no sympathy whatever.'

Evans' team had carried on above Crowley's old camp. Their subsequent siege of the summit was made hard by the serrated ridge above them; to avoid this, they hoped to carve out a route up the South-West Face of the mountain. At the time, the accepted wisdom was that the giant Himalayan peaks could only be climbed by their ridges, so this was a bold move.

It paid off. Almost to their surprise, they found a line up the face that put them within striking distance of the top. George and Joe Brown were chosen as the lead climbers to make the summit attempt on 25 May 1955. Their last camp was at around 27,000 feet. They fortified themselves beforehand with a breakfast of orangeade, tea, asparagus soup, canned lamb's tongue and mashed potato. Brown noted ruefully: 'Thinking that it would be impossible to smoke at this altitude, I had brought only five cigarettes. But I found that so long as I sat still, I could enjoy smoking as much as ever, and wished that I had taken a full packet.'

Brown's rock-climbing expertise came in useful near the top, where there was a last, difficult pitch – 'quite tricky', in George's usual, understated description – where Brown led the way up a crack with an overhang in it. And then they had stopped short of the summit itself.

To me, this was one of the most admirable moments in mountaineering history. George and Joe Brown did not climb onto the summit, which was a few feet above them, simply because the Sikkimese had asked them not to. There was a strong Buddhist sentiment that no venerated peak should be climbed.

This was not a condition that they had been forced to accept – they were climbing from the Nepalese side of the mountain anyway. For two young climbers to stop short, after one of the toughest climbs in the world, was exemplary. George laconically told me: 'Of course, it gave us a good excuse not to do the last little bit.'

Brown described his feelings at the time: 'One expects to be overwhelmed by a terrific feeling of triumph at the top of a mountain, especially one as big as Kangchenjunga. Now we felt only relief at not having to step up again and also a great feeling of peace and tranquillity. After spending so long on a mountain one tends to lose sight of the fact that there is a top and the point of the expedition is to get there.'

Their example was followed elsewhere: two years later, Jimmy Roberts's expedition to climb Machhapuchhare again stopped short some 150 feet below the summit, and they petitioned the Nepalese Government to leave the peak sacrosanct. No permits have been allowed for it since.

Back on Kangchenjunga, the first expedition to climb the peak from the Sikkimese side in 1977, an Indian one led by none other than 'Bull' Kumar, also respected the sanctity of the summit. In 1979, the shock troopers of the

Bonington years, Doug Scott, Peter Boardman and Joe Tasker, halted below the crest as well. 'But then,' said George sadly, 'a Japanese expedition came along and trampled all over the top.'

Such subtleties have been lost altogether in today's supremacist climbing culture. How fast, how high, how little oxygen you need, how 'hard' you are – these are now the only parameters to respect. Even Ginette Harrison, in 1998 the first woman to ascend Kangchenjunga, planted her ice axe firmly on the summit, ignoring any local sentiments.

In the years since that first ascent of Kangchenjunga, it was Joe Brown himself and his climbing partner, Don Whillans, who were largely responsible for the cult of the 'hard', in which all that matters is having a brew, and conversations are for soft Southern buggers. In his autobiography, called, of course, *The Hard Years* (on the cover of which Joe is smoking a cigarette), Brown says admiringly of Don Whillans: 'He exemplified more than anyone in British mountaineering the image of a "hard man".' Whillans was notorious for having, when only fifteen, knocked out a bus conductor who had had the temerity to demand an extra halfpenny fare from him.

Chris Bonington ruefully recounts a story when he was climbing with Don Whillans on the North Face of the Eiger. Whillans turned to him and said: 'I'll meet any bugger halfway, but don't expect me to go further.'

This cult of the taciturn was extended by Peter Boardman and Joe Tasker ('We had to stay within our shell to do this climb,' as Boardman put it when climbing

Changabang) and had become the defining characteristic of a school of British climbing, along with cropped hair and a survivalist approach. The good climber, went this line, travelled light, both in terms of equipment and emotions.

The 'hard man of few words who just gets the job done' approach might originally have been designed to challenge the old 'officer class' methods of the Alpine Club, but its long-term consequences have been unfortunate. How far it has gone can be seen from a comparison of two accounts of expeditions to the Nanda Devi Sanctuary, one by a British expedition in 1978, the other by Indian mountaineers in 1961.

On the British expedition, Terry King and Paul Lloyd spend a masochistic seven days trying unsuccessfully to climb the North Face of Nanda Devi Alpine-style, bivouacking in impossible places and only interrupting their day at the rock face for a mug of tea and a muttered word of conversation. They are accompanied by two hapless Indian Liaison Officers, whom they consistently make fun of and then leave behind. It amuses them to call Bangue, the Sikh officer accompanying them, 'Bango'; they laugh when the other officer, Bali, falls into a glacier. The tone is that of British package-holiday travellers abroad, with continual complaints about the weather, interspersed with discussions about the possibility of mosquitoes at that altitude (manifestly absurd) and whether they should take their malaria tablets.

Terry King's later report of the expedition is relentlessly 'hard' and joyless; the account of their slow progress up the North Face is broken only by the incessant brews of tea the two prepare. They seem hardly to talk to one another. At one point there is an argument because the teaspoon gets lost. In a startlingly revealing aside, King writes proudly: 'We sustained the upward drive with crude, mindless determination, void of inner feelings . . .'

Their experiences at the end of the expedition may account for this. King and Lloyd were unlucky enough to be climbing when strange reports of a possible CIA expedition to Nanda Devi were made public, so they were taken into custody on suspicion of spying and escorted to Joshimath for questioning. Later, they were released without charge. But their overall attitude is still unredeemed by the slightest interest in the country around them. The North Face of Nanda Devi is a climbing challenge that happens, inconveniently, to be in the middle of the Himalaya. They look forward to returning to 'the comforts of the Western World'.

Compare this to the Indian mountaineer Hari Dang's description of an expedition to the Sanctuary with Gurdial Singh and John Dias in 1961. They too have a hard time getting in, being beaten back from the Dharansi pass by an avalanche. But the Sanctuary, once reached, is just that – a haven and an overwhelming experience for the climbers: 'We spent many days oblivious of the world of compulsion, in a State of Grace.' They roam delightedly across it, attempting less than the British climbers – no first routes here – but seeming to take away more. The accent is on spontaneity, exploration and enjoyment.

One night they decide to climb Trisuli by moonlight,

from the north. As they climb they see 'an ultra-violet sea of light absorbing the light over the Inner Sanctuary'. To either side of Nanda Devi, 'strung out as on a clothes line', are 'the ultimate mountains of the world: Hanuman, Changabang, Kalanka, Trisuli'. The mood is transcendental: 'the light transformed the mountains into an orange crystal in which we saw everything ... A flaming torch as big as the summit platform of Nanda Devi detached itself from the peak and moved silently and smoothly, like the shadow of a flying eagle, across the arête towards the east.'

Hari Dang summarises the experience: 'Men are born human. They become mountaineers. Restlessness is their fate.' The modern 'hard' school of British mountaineering would probably sneer at this as greeting-card philosophy – but I had no doubts to which school Eric Shipton belonged. As an explorer as well as a mountaineer, his sympathies would have been with the Indians, as indeed were mine.

*

It was very late before everyone reached the campsite. Alan Tate, an experienced potholer who had apparently explored some tough systems, was knocked out by both altitude and a virulent head cold, a bad combination. He took thirteen hours to complete the journey, arriving shortly before midnight, and looked in a bad way. Natalena Dacunha was carried down by porters who slung her unceremoniously between them, holding the flaming torches of birch bark in their teeth. The cumulative ascent (which George Band, with his meticulous habits, had measured to be some 3,700 feet) tested those whose knees were vulnerable, but it was not the distance nor the height that was causing problems.

Some of those on the expedition had done a great deal of British trekking but nothing at any altitude. There is a commonly held but dangerous view that if you can hack it on Snowdon or the Peak District, you should be fine on similar-grade climbs in the Himalaya – the attitude with which the young Joe Brown set out from Manchester to climb Kangchenjunga. For Brown it held true. For many it doesn't.

The last of the stragglers limped down from the hillside above, looking exhausted. When our bags finally turned up, I rummaged around until my numb fingers closed on the plastic miniature bottles of Absolut Vodka and toasted the anonymous Swedish air hostess in the dark of my tent, before falling into a deep and dreamless sleep.

The next morning a rest day was declared.

We needed it. Illness had swept though the group: Mac, Loreto and various others seemed to have caught the same heavy respiratory cold that Alan had been suffering from; George had stomach problems; and some climbers were still exhausted from the day before.

Mountains are not healthy places. On the American expedition to Nanda Devi in 1976, the team members variously contracted hepatitis, spinal meningitis and expedysentery; one woman was taken off the mountain by helicopter with altitude problems and another died from them. On my return from one trip to the Himalaya with severe vestibulitis, an acute and irritating infection of the nose, the specialist consultant summoned his students around me and said, with relish: 'Ah yes, acute vestibulitis, often suffered by those who spend time at high altitudes. It is completely incurable.'

The unscheduled rest day was not popular with the porters. For some arcane and counter-productive reason, porters in this part of the Himalaya arrange to be paid not by the day, but by how many stages of a journey they have made. So a rest day is a lost day. Under this system, porters will always want to press on regardless. Akshay had his hands full placating them.

Steve Berry, a bridge player, gathered a hard core of enthusiasts round him in the tent. I joined him, Bull and George for a hand or two, but by evening was sitting outside with the porters around the large bonfire they had lit; it was warmer and they were a jovial bunch, despite their irritation at the rest day. They too were playing cards, for wagers of two, four or six rupees. One told me: 'With cards, time passes, time passes.'

I liked the fierce heat of the fire and the way the porters' skins glowed red against it, the intense smell of juniper burning and the odd crack of wood breaking, the long silences and the sudden quick interchanges. The fire had been made using fallen wood, but one of the problems about access to the Sanctuary was that such fires, particularly above the tree-line, can have a devastating effect on the juniper scrub when lit on more than an occasional basis. If the Sanctuary were to be opened up, kerosene would need to be carried in and porter shelters built.

I noticed that the Liaison Officer from the Forestry Department, a self-effacing man called Bimal, had quietly joined the group. He had seemed overawed by Bull and the international team, and had as yet hardly said a word, but he knew much about the forest, as one of the few people ever allowed to visit it.

To my surprise, the head man or *pradhan* of Lata village suddenly stumbled into the clearing and marched up to the Liaison Officer. In a loud, declamatory voice he said: 'I have just come from Lata. I have no permit to come into this restricted area. What are you going to do about it?' Bimal looked embarrassed and stared into the fire, before slipping away. The porters were delighted.

It was not the first time that the *pradhan* had deliberately tried to provoke the authorities into arresting him. Earlier in the year he had led a mass trespass from Lata into the restricted area. A contingent of armed police had been sent to chase the villagers back out. The *pradhan* had been quoted in local papers as saying that, despite this, one day they 'would swoop and take their rights'.

The *pradhan* talked to me about the injustices of the present system. The village was right on the edge of the restricted zone. They could not gain access to their grazing or traditional medicines – like the angelica that grew all around us. Before its closure in 1982, they had depended on getting into the extended Nanda Devi Sanctuary area for the eight months of the year when the passes were open. At the time, the government had promised them alternative grazing grounds to the north, near Badrinath. This had come to nothing.

....

Slowly he fell silent, as did the rest of the group, and we all stared into the fire. Above, the snow on the great face of Mount Hanuman shone luminously in the moonlight.

*

That night I dreamt of the Tounot. The Tounot was the first mountain I climbed as a boy. It was only 10,500 feet, but had a satisfyingly savage northern face, which dominated the small Alpine village of St Luc where we were staying. And it had an even more satisfying approach up around the back, avoiding that savage face but emerging on top of it.

This approach took you into a 'hidden valley', a world with its own small lakes, curious terminal moraines and deserted shepherds' huts. As a boy of thirteen, it was a perfect place to escape. The way into it was by a small glen that curled under a serrated ridge called the Pointes de Nava. The Val du Tounot itself was virtually unvisited, as it led nowhere and was too high for good pasture.

For me it was the first mountain area I could make my own, a private place signifying, in the phrase Eric Shipton used in his autobiography, 'that untravelled world' which I wanted to explore. My parents, who would have been reluctant to let me loose on the nightlife of London, were quite happy for me to roam the Alps on my own, and I spent days criss-crossing this small valley, with its mountain gentians, soldanella growing on the snowline and lakes of an improbably intense blue.

It was some time before I tried climbing the mountain

itself. This was not because of any great difficulty – a way led up in broad zigzags and was a matter of perseverance rather than agility – but rather I felt a reluctance to follow it, a feeling that I might devalue what I had created in the 'hidden valley'.

When I did emerge on the summit, there was an impressive view. The village of St Luc lay directly beneath me, south-facing and taking the afternoon sun. I could see the main Val d'Anniviers below, with the Rhône valley in the distance and the whole of the Pennine Alps sweeping down to meet it.

Yet when I returned to my little valley, it suddenly felt diminished, in shadow from the mountain and a stony grey compared to the sunlit meadows I had just seen far below on the other side. From then on, I lost any appetite for the idea of reaching summits. More enjoyable was to cross a high mountain pass and move into a new, yielding perspective of other mountains and other paths. To summit seemed an arid achievement.

Only once did I enjoy being on top of a mountain and in my dream I segued forward to this moment, a moment that had always had great resonance for me.

I stood on the top of Fleetwith Pike in the Lake District in the early morning. Below me, coming up the Honister pass and fanning out, were the hunters. I stood deliberately on the very top of the peak so that they could see me silhouetted. Then I blew the horn. The noise carried and echoed off across to Great Gable, Haystacks, Kirkfell. And the hunters started moving with greater purpose up towards me. I turned and ran back off the Pike and along the narrow ridge that drops down sharply towards Buttermere lake. I ran as I had never run before, with the adrenaline and the horn beating against my chest. I could no longer see the hunters, but I knew they were behind me. Buttermere seemed to be under my feet, but was a mile away. It felt as if I were running off the top of the world.

The hunters followed me and although I could no longer see them I could hear their voices over the bluff of the hill, echoing in the slate quarries of the Honister pass. Of course the hunt was a game. But then again it wasn't.

For many years I had participated in the fell-running 'manhunts' that take place in the Western Fells of the Lake District, where a few runners are selected to be chased down by the rest of the pack. That memory of Fleetwith Pike was the memory that always came back to me in dreams.

I woke up and went out to join the porters again. They were huddled around the fire that was still burning through the night. One offered me a cigarette.

I thought that what mountaineers really want is to be alone in the mountains, but with other people who also like being alone.

*

We set off the next morning in brilliant sunshine. The hillside was full of cotoneaster, piptanthus, azaleas and tiny blue cyananthus flowers.

I got talking to one of the cooks, a Kashmiri called Walia

Mohammed, as we walked along. 'Is Kashmir as beautiful as this?' I asked. I had never been there.

Walia looked sad. 'Kashmir used to be heaven, but now no longer,' he said, looking out over the valley: 'Too much trouble in the world.'

We were behind a large group of porters as we trekked up the lower gorge towards Nanda Devi. The gorge here was not as narrow or as dangerous as it would later become, but there were some exposed ledges in that dangerous grey area between being just manageable and needing fixed ropes. I heard a shout. When I ran forward and came around a buttress, I saw the porters all looking down a cliff face ahead, gesticulating.

My first thought was that someone had fallen. When I reached the group, I found Steve Berry already with them. 'It's only a bag,' he told me. One of the porters had been carrying it on his shoulder going round a rock ledge; the bag had caught on an overhang and had fallen down the cliff. The porter had only just let go of it in time and had been lucky not to fall himself. I looked down at the drop to the Rishi Ganges, thousands of feet below.

My relief was momentary. 'The thing is, Hugh,' said Steve gently, 'we think it was *your* bag.'

He let this sink in for a moment. 'It was black – and you're the only one with a black bag.'

This was true. We had all been issued with matching orange canvas bags to put our kit in. In a cantankerous way I had refused, being attached to the black synthetic canoe sack I had used in the Andes for years. Although it looked more like a body bag than luggage, I knew it was completely rip-proof; the canvas bags that we were issued with wouldn't even keep out the water. And I have always hated a uniform.

That morning I had been faced with the daily choice: to carry most of the camera gear and films safely with me or to put them in this black bag to go ahead with the porters. As usually happened, my interior dialogue went as follows: 'You really should carry all your spare gear and film stock around with you.' To be answered: 'Get a life. I'm more likely to go over the side than the porters are. And the stuff weighs too much.'

Now my *karma* had caught up with me. I was clearly a lightweight, with no professionalism, who deserved this.

Steve pointed to a short section of fixed rope, which I hadn't noticed. It lay across the near-vertical rock cliff and led down. 'Deva's gone to look for it.'

'He can't go down that!' But he already had. I could see him far below, slithering, slipping and jumping from ledges to the small bushes that grew out of the cracks. It was the most vertiginous drop I'd ever seen a man descend without protection. 'It's not worth it, Steve. Really.'

I watched, feeling weak. We were close to a waterfall and Deva was by now too far down to hear us. We followed him through Steve's binoculars, silhouetted against the Rishi Ganges a mile below. He disappeared behind a bluff and re-emerged, clutching a small black bag by the straps.

I was puzzled, as it looked far too small to be mine. 'Jesus,' said Steve, 'it's not yours at all. It's Loreto's personal bag.'

Loreto had a small black bag that she used for her

personal stuff – we had teased her by calling it a make-up bag. It made sense. I had been wondering how the hell the porter had been able to carry my much larger and heavier bag on his shoulders, rather than across his back.

Deva started to come back up. He reached a small rock wall, which gave him trouble – whichever way he tried to get round it, he was blocked. Finally, when he tried virtually to vault it, the straps of the black bag gave way and it fell again, this time bursting open and spewing its contents out down the cliff towards the river, like confetti.

Deva banged his hand angrily on the rock and looked up at Steve, as if to say, 'What do I do now?' Steve waved him up.

Just then Loreto came round the corner. Now it was my turn to tell her that her bag had gone over the side. Her face crumpled. I knew exactly how she felt.

*

The first time I saw the High Himalaya was out of an aeroplane window, flying from Kathmandu to Paro in Bhutan, one of the most spectacular flights in the world.

It was my first day in the Himalaya. And already there was Everest close on the port side, looking benign and stately, with Lhotse, Makalu and Cho Oyu peeling away as a line of 8,000-metre peaks to either side. I knew their names because the pilot identified them over the tannoy.

It was absurdly easy, overfamiliar, like taking a coach trip around these geological dinosaurs, a Cretaceous theme park to remind the traveller of a time when the world had places so inhospitable that man could not survive there.

Only now that we were approaching under the belly of one of these beasts could I appreciate their true scale. To get to the box canyon that protects the Nanda Devi Sanctuary would take at least seven days of awkwardly picking our way around the shoulders and deep gorges that surrounded the mountain. We would occasionally get glimpses of Nanda Devi, but often it would be hidden by those gorges or by cloud. This was the way you got to know a mountain, from different angles, obliquely and with respect. This was real time.

Our next campsite was at a place called Deodi, just the other side of the river. From there I was able to climb up a small tributary stream to a cliff bluff created by a waterfall and get a perfect sight line of the mountain, which, unusually for the evening, was not hidden by clouds.

As it was sunset, the West Face of Nanda Devi was lit up. The nearby wisps of cloud were moving fast, and the mountain seemed to change its aspect every second in a coquettish way as I took roll after roll of film. 'Oh baby, give it to me one more time,' I muttered, in a cultural reference to *Austin Powers* which Bishen may not have picked up on as he struggled to hold the tripod steady on the precipitous slope.

But if Nanda Devi had so far been elusive, there was another mountain that I wanted to see even more: Changabang, the famous 'shining mountain'. This lay within the Sanctuary. Until now it had been completely invisible and it looked as if it would remain so; the deep gorges would give no natural line of vision to it at any point on our journey.

John Shipton and I discovered from Shanka, one of the older porters, that there was a site much higher on the mountainside above us where, he claimed, we could obtain a view of Changabang across the Rhamani glacier. The rest of the group were disinclined to believe him – 'He just wants a tip' – but we signed up to try to see it early next day.

John was in an unusually garrulous mood as we set off, perhaps because he was freed from his usual responsibilities as trek leader. He told me about his chequered education: he had been expelled first from public school, then from grammar school, before throwing a bucket of water over his dean at university and being expelled from that as well. He had ended up studying the unexpectedly sober subject of economics at a polytechnic, before taking off around the world teaching English.

He had never known Eric well. His father had left home when he was young, chasing mountains and women, and John had always found it difficult to be close to him. At one point his mother, worried that father and son were not communicating, had persuaded Eric to take John up Mount Disgrazia in Italy, a climb that Eric had first made as a young man.

Much later, Eric had taken John to see an old lady before a climb; she had looked at them both and said: 'Where are you two young men going off to in such a hurry?' John had suddenly felt a frisson of shared destiny, a feeling that they were essentially alike. Likewise, Eric had arranged for John to crew for Tilman on one of Tilman's epic sailing voyages, and had asked, confidingly, on John's return, 'what he had thought of Bill?'

But it was clear that things had never been easy between father and son. When Eric died in 1977, John was in Africa and only heard about his death months later. Only in the past few years had he begun obsessively to retrace his father's legacy, visiting Mount Burney in Patagonia and some of the sites in the Garhwal that Eric had explored. And now he had come to the site of perhaps his father's greatest achievement, the Nanda Devi Sanctuary.

While John was talking, Shanka led us on a circuitous route high above Deodi and the Trisul Nala. Bishen spotted some angelica as we passed and uprooted it, as it was supposed to have healing powers, particularly for the stomach.

It was a beautiful if wild scramble. However, there was precious little sign of Changabang and Shanka had a disconcerting habit of continually retracing his steps. Bishen and I were beginning to lose faith in his abilities: 'No good guide, no good guide,' Bishen kept repeating in a loud whisper designed to be heard by the man himself. Shanka was looking rattled. Like the White Rabbit in *Alice in Wonderland*, he was sure he had left the mountain somewhere around here.

But then he pulled it out of his hat, from the middle of a path that had fallen away in a landslide and so confused him. With the precision of a sniper's rifle, we had a clear view up the gorge of the Rhamani glacier to Changabang.

I always hesitate to call any mountain 'beautiful' – it is

difficult to call anything beautiful that has the potential to kill – but Changabang is so perfect a peak that it is difficult not to. 'A shark's tooth of granite thrusting into the skies' in Chris Bonington's words, it reminded me of the Chrysler Building in New York.

The 'shining mountain' is one of the most mythologised and least seen in mountaineering history. Ever since the first Victorians had come across it, Changabang had been held up as the perfect peak, to rank with the Matterhorn in Europe. Here is how W.H. 'Bill' Murray rhapsodised about it in his characteristically lyrical, Scottish way: 'As fragile as an icicle; a product of earth and sky rare and fantastic, and of liveliness unparalleled so that unaware one's pulse leapt and the heart gave thanks that this mountain should be as it is.'

To me, Changabang looked as if it had been airbrushed against the sky as a fantasy mountain, rather than being made up of stones, rock and grit. It was even more difficult to believe that it had been climbed. When Bull had flown over the Sanctuary in 1964, this was the peak that had caught his eye – 'the formidable yellow and black spire of Changabang, still unclimbed, and no wonder'. But in 1974 it was finally conquered by an Anglo-Indian expedition led by Bonington and Balwhant Sandhu. In those years Bonington spent considerable time in the Garhwal between his Everest adventures, rather as the Indian mountaineers had done in the sixties.

The most memorable description of Changabang had been left by Peter Boardman and Joe Tasker, who put the first route up the daunting West Face a few years later in

1976. This was then considered to be one of the hardest climbs ever undertaken in the Himalaya.

Boardman and Tasker were the *enfants terribles* of British climbing in the seventies. In some ways the Shipton and Tilman of their day, they often quoted Shipton as an influence on their own similar style of lightweight, two-man mountaineering. And, like Shipton, they instinctively disliked the big expedition; Boardman had described Bonington's huge 1975 assault on Everest, in which he had taken part, as 'the last great colonial experience'.

For this mission impossible, they decided to go in on their own, Alpine style. From our position, I could see the West Face that they had scaled, a sheer side of granite and ice that many of their contemporaries had declared unclimbable. Their attempt on Changabang was perhaps their finest hour and it certainly produced their finest book, called, naturally, *The Shining Mountain* (written by Boardman with interpolations from Tasker).

The assault was epic. They had special sling-bivouacs designed for them so that they could sleep hanging from the rock face. It took seven days of nightmarish pitches to get to the summit. Competitiveness drove them on. They seem to have exchanged fewer words than Bodie and Doyle in *The Professionals*, each wrapped in a separate world.

Because they were climbing the West Face, Nanda Devi was hidden from view. But when they finally got to the top of Changabang, they were able to look down into what Boardman described as 'the Sanctuary of my childhood dreams':

And there it was. Nanda Devi, the bliss-giving Goddess. Clouds plumed horizontally from its summit above its shadowed North-Eastern Walls. These 8,000-foot walls formed a vast, forbidding amphitheatre of swirling mist. To the west, however, the sun picked out a silver track along the Northern Ridge that threaded its way to the main summit. And the summit was clear. Below the spaciousness between our spire and the twin-peaked mass of Nanda Devi, stretched the upper arms of the promised land . . . It was the 15th of October and winter would soon cover all that wilderness. No man slept there.

Six years later, in 1982, Peter Boardman and Joe Tasker died together on the North-East ridge of Everest. They were last seen by Chris Bonington heading up towards the summit. The approach to Everest from the north had already claimed the lives of Mallory and Irvine in the twenties, and countless more since; Shipton had his closest call on a reconnaissance there in 1936, when an avalanche nearly took him with it.

I felt an unreasoning dislike of Everest as I stared at Changabang. Compared to the elegant impossibility of Changabang, Everest was a brute of a mountain: in Louis MacNeice's phrase, 'aloof, inviolate, murderous'.

*

I had by now a routine for the evening: an hour in a sleeping bag, writing or listening to a tape; then a wander over to the mess tent, which would already be lit up by the head-torches inside, casting large shadows on the canvas. A huddle of people would be crouched over the table, playing cards, eating or spinning tales late into the night.

As the journey progressed, these stories being traded in the camps became as important to me as the landscape we trekked through during the day. Before his death, Michael Aris, the distinguished Bhutan scholar, had told me of the Buddhist tradition of *terma*, the hidden texts left in the mountains by sages to be rediscovered by later generations. This tradition had recently been resurgent in Tibet, where these rediscovered *terma* were often the focus of Buddhist opposition to Chinese rule, a reaffirmation that the land itself resisted the invaders, that the land spoke back. And increasingly I was finding that here in the Nanda Devi Sanctuary, in an area supposedly unoccupied and unexplored, there were a surprising number of other hidden texts to discover myself.

That evening Natalena Dacunha told me a particularly strange story. I had heard odd rumours of it before, but aside from an oblique editorial note in a recent republication of Shipton's and Tilman's acounts of Nanda Devi, and Bill Aitken's cryptic comments, it had seemed too bizarre to take much credence of. Natalena, like many on the expedition, was an obsessive bibliophile and she had first come across the story while trawling the Internet; I later confirmed it from other sources.

The story made sense of much that had puzzled me. Above all, it answered the question of why the Sanctuary had been closed by the Indian Government.

inset: W.W. Graham and Tom Longstaff, two of the early mountaineers who unsuccessfully attempted to enter the Nanda Devi Sanctuary.

main picture: Tom Longstaff's 1905 photograph of the twin peaks of Nanda Devi and the walls of the Sanctuary from the south-east.

Eric Shipton: *'a wanderer who enjoyed the highways and byways, but was not obsessed by the need to plant a flag on the top of a mountain'*.

Eric Shipton and H.W. 'Bill' Tilman setting off for Nanda Devi in 1934: *'Temperamentally, Shipton and Tilman could not have been more different.'*

Shipton on Nanda Devi.

Shipton and Tilman with the Sherpas on the 1934 expedition: (*left to right*) Angtharkay, Shipton, Pasang, Tilman and Kusang.

'*The great North Wall of Nanda Devi: one of the most gigantic mountain faces in the world, standing 8000 ft above the glacier – a mountain partly scaled by Mr Shipton's expedition.*': The photograph and caption used by the *Illustrated London News* in 1935 for Shipton's first published account of Nanda Devi.

Shipton's photograph of the northern side of the Sanctuary, showing the peaks protecting it, with Changabang on the left.

Topographical illustration of the Sanctuary, originally used by Eric Shipton in *Nanda Devi* (1936).

Narinder 'Bull' Kumar: *'For twenty years between 1960 and 1981 he led a series of expeditions that were sometimes controversial but undeniably brave'*. In 1964, his team made the second ascent of Mount Nanda Devi.

Willi Unsoeld and his daughter Nanda Devi just before their 1976 expedition to the mountain.

After the 1962 Indo-China War, the CIA determined to keep a close watch on Chinese activities on the Sinkiang plateau. In 1964 this became more urgent when China detonated its first atomic bomb. So in 1965 the CIA decided (and one would have thought that even Dr Strangelove would have baulked at such a plan) to plant a nuclear-powered spying device on the summit of Nanda Devi, as a suitably high point near the Tibetan border. They hoped the device would be able to monitor the radio transmissions controlling any Chinese rocket launches. These findings would be relayed to a CIA agent based about thirty miles away, in a 'Field Research Unit (FRU)' at Sandev. The idea had presumably arisen because Bull and his Indian team had successfully reached the summit of Nanda Devi the year before.

The CIA seems to have had no idea of the difficulty of what they were proposing. They recruited some of America's top mountaineers, including members of the successful 1963 American expedition to Everest, and took them to Langley in Virginia. After being sworn to secrecy and signing non-disclosure agreements, they were given extensive and apparently tedious briefings on how to assemble a nuclear-powered device. They were also promised wages of $1,000 a month, which was a lot of money for impoverished mountaineers to do what many had anyway always dreamt of: go to Nanda Devi.

Realising that to plant such a radioactive machine by the headwaters of India's most important river might not go down well with the Indian Government, the CIA covertly approached Indian military intelligence, the CBI, which agreed to become involved on an 'unofficial, non-attributable' basis. The CBI even volunteered to supply some Indian climbers to help with the project. And not just any climbers. Some of the Indian team who had just successfully climbed Everest found themselves being drafted into a military unit to help the Americans. They were put under the command of their leader on Everest, Captain Mohan Kohli, but I was relieved to discover that Bull, who had been his deputy leader on Everest, was not involved.

The joint Indo-American team went off to practise climbing together on a face of the formidable Mount McKinley, which the CIA had arranged to be roped off for them; the climb failed, a forerunner of what was to come.

By the autumn of 1965, the team were assembled in India and trying to operate in total secrecy, although taking a full expedition into the Nanda Devi Sanctuary can hardly have been an inconspicuous undertaking. The Indian intelligence service, worried that the Americans might give themselves away, instructed the climbers 'to keep their faces averted and their conversation restricted to monosyllables'. The Americans were also asked to use an Indian fake suntan lotion called 'Man-Tan' to darken their skins. The operation was code-named 'Blue Mountain'. The Americans were referred to as 'friends', the Indians as 'members'. If the results of the mission had not been so destructive, the plan would have made the perfect plot for a sixties caper movie. All they needed was for Q to issue them with accelerating ice axes.

While the Indian climbers had to get there on foot, the

Americans were flown into the Sanctuary by helicopter. The nuclear-powered device was carried into the Sanctuary by porters, who were told it was treasure of some sort, possibly gold. The CIA had arranged more cover for the project: the climbers were to pretend that they were studying the effects of low oxygen supplies on the body as part of a 'High Altitude Test (HAT) programme'. The generator itself, measuring about two by three feet and shaped like a mushroom, was called Space Nuclear Auxiliary Power or SNAP for short.

So with enough acronyms to keep their CIA minders happy for months, the team set off up Nanda Devi. With some difficulty, as the attempt had been left to the last few weeks before winter, the climbers managed to get the device to within 2,500 feet of the summit. But then bad weather forced them to retreat. Rather than carry the heavy SNAP back down with them, they hid it on the mountainside.

At the heart of the device was a fuel-rod containing plutonium-238, capable of driving the machine for seventy-five years. Plutonium-238 is a nuclear synthetic that loses heat as it decays.

Next year, in the spring of 1966, the Indian mountaineers were sent back on their own to finish the job. To their horror, they discovered that a large landslide had covered the nuclear-powered device. It was completely lost. They reported this back to their understandably alarmed superiors at Indian intelligence, who in turn told the CIA ('I am sorry to say we may be experiencing a small operational problem with Project Blue Mountain'). The

CIA sent another team of American mountaineers back to India with some rescue helicopters, while they tried to think of a solution to the problem.

The climbers had been expressly forbidden to do any mountaineering unless strictly necessary. Left idle in the Sanctuary, bored and with unclimbed peaks all around them, they began to mutiny. The interdict became impossible to enforce with such an elite squad. An Indian climber, Gurcharan Bhangu, and an American, Robert Schaller, at different times made solo ascents of Nanda Devi itself, which had never been done – indeed, the peak had only been climbed twice before. These must still stand as some of the most audacious ascents ever made on Nanda Devi, even though they are unrecorded in any mountaineering gazette, and were undertaken in the knowledge that the climbers would not receive any publicity or glory from being successful. In an odd way, the decidedly dirty actions of the CIA had resulted in some of the 'purest' climbs ever made in the Himalaya.

Meanwhile the big brains at Langley came up with a brilliant idea. The team was to buy up all the fire hose they could, attach it to a mountain stream and try to flush away the debris that covered the nuclear-powered device.

This farcical idea was actually attempted before even the CIA realised that the resultant pressure of water would hardly move a sandcastle, let alone the substantial rock-pile left by the avalanche. So they then decided simply to bury the idea. The device was left where it was. The Indian intelligence services were easily bullied into keeping quiet about it – they were, after all, already complicit. The CIA also entertained a paranoid conspiracy theory that the Indians had really stolen the pocket nuclear generator to kick-start their own nuclear programme.

All this time the Chinese were indeed building launching pads for their nuclear missiles in Sinkiang, due north of Nanda Devi, at one point in 1966 even launching a test rocket from a base in central Sinkiang, unobserved by the CIA.

In desperation the CIA decided to mount another tracking device, this time on Nanda Kot, a lower neighbour of Nanda Devi at 22,500 feet. With what must have been a soothing pretence that there was some logic to all this, the new mission was code-named 'Operation Red Mountain'. The expedition set off in 1967 and, despite a near-fatal avalanche that almost killed Captain Kohli, managed to install the device near the summit.

Any self-congratulation back at Langley was short-lived. The device stopped transmitting during the winter and yet another Indian team had to be sent up in the spring of 1968 to find out why. The assumption was that it had simply clogged up with snow.

What the Indian climbers and the accompanying Sherpas found was chilling: the heat of the nuclear generator had caused it to sink far down into the ice dome on the summit of Nanda Kot. The ice had then re-formed over the top again. When the team dug deep into the ice, they came across the shaft that the generator had left behind in its descent, and followed it below with torches. At the bottom of the shaft, they found the generator sitting in a cavity it had created for itself; the ice walls were five feet away, and had been carved into strange shapes by the constant melting and freezing. One of them described it as being like 'a religious icon in a cathedral of ice'. With difficulty, they carried the generator back up to the surface and waited for an American helicopter to land and reclaim it.

The irony was that such devices had already been superseded. A new surveillance satellite was launched, which did the job of monitoring Chinese rockets much better from space.

The CIA moved on. But the nuclear-powered device that they had left buried on the slopes of Nanda Devi remained. And any attempt to keep the story secret was doomed to failure. Mountaineers have plenty of time to swap stories, precisely as we had been doing, and 'non-disclosure agreements' don't mean much when you're sharing a tent at altitude. Over the course of the four years that the CIA had mounted expeditions in the Garhwal, they had used most of the cream of American mountaineering talent, including no less than five members of the 1963 Dyhrenfurth expedition to Everest. One of the coordinators of the CIA team was Barry Bishop, who had reached the summit of Everest in 1963 and whose close association with *National Geographic* magazine as a photographer gave him the perfect cover for foreign travel.

By the end of the sixties it was one of the best-known 'secrets' of the Himalaya among climbers. And in the post-Vietnam fallout of the seventies, it was soon published. In 1978, the American climbing magazine *Outside* produced a sketchy account, without naming the climbers involved.

There was uproar in India, with demonstrations both inside and outside Parliament. Prime Minister Desai's government had to respond. It did so, characteristically, by blaming the previous administration of Indira Gandhi for the problem and by going into denial. First they arrested the members of various expeditions who were unlucky enough to find themselves in the Sanctuary at the time. Then in 1982 the Sanctuary was closed to all visitors, supposedly for environmental reasons to preserve the ecology.

The one military expedition that the government has since allowed to enter the Sanctuary has been made up of Indian Army sappers, not previously known for their mountaineering expertise; in their bland official report, they talked of the need to 'clean up the Sanctuary', although the presumption must be that they carried Geiger counters rather than litter-sticks to do so.

Meanwhile the buried plutonium-238 sits somewhere under the rocks of Nanda Devi. Plutonium-238 remains radioactive for between 300 and 500 years. The outer shell of the SNAP generator will corrode long before that, releasing radioactive materials close to one of the sources of the Ganges. For once, the phrase 'time bomb' seemed appropriate. It was a sobering thought.

Recently there have been rumours that some of the surviving Indian members of the CIA-sponsored expeditions are suffering from radioactive-related diseases. In the consequent disquiet, there has been more readiness to talk about the events of forty years ago. In particular, there is some bitterness that the American climbers refused to handle the device; by contrast, the Indians did most of the load-carrying.

Indeed, the Indian porters on the approach routes actually liked carrying the SNAP because of the heat that the decaying plutonium-238 gave off. They affectionately christened it 'Padmasambhava', after the legendary Buddhist sage who was said to have flown over the Himalaya on a tiger, and who left influential hidden texts, *terma*, for later generations to discover.

*

Much to our own porters' disgust, we had another enforced rest day at Deodi. This was because of an accommodation blockage in the gorge; the Indo-Tibetan Border Police team were now coming back out of the Sanctuary and had taken the campsite we would next require, at Rhamani.

The ITBP were a mixed blessing. Whilst they had partially reopened the Sanctuary, by building a log-bridge across the Rishi and leaving, we hoped, some fixed-rope routes along the cliffs of the gorge, they had also brought a hundred porters and left considerable rubbish behind. The ITBP had also carved their initials on some of the trees. Steve Berry was so angry when we arrived at the Deodi camp and found litter everywhere that he threw some at the ITBP men in their nearby tent. Bull went in later and diplomatically smoothed over the incident, before we were evicted.

I had no problem with another rest day. I got an

unheard-of nine hours' uninterrupted sleep (like Shipton, I liked to lie in if at all possible) and the sun was still shining.

Himalayan weather is complicated. There are only two brief 'windows' that give safe access to the mountains: the spring season, between the winter snows and the monsoon, and the autumn, when the monsoon has cleared. The conventional thinking was that spring was the best of these windows, and so all the great early Himalayan campaigns had taken place then. But, as Bull commented, you could end up racing the monsoon, which in the last few years has become increasingly unpredictable, along with all global weather systems. Better by far to come safely after the rains, in the autumn, as we had done – although the corollary is that you then have to race the returning winter snows. And already there was a hint of cold blowing in.

When Shipton and Tilman had come, they had typically used both seasons – the first in the spring of 1934 to force a way up the gorge, the second in the autumn to explore the Sanctuary once they'd found a way in. And between those campaigns, just to keep in shape, right in the middle of the monsoon, they had forced a passage over the Badrinath and Kedarnath watershed, a hair-raising journey through new territory. Not for nothing had Bonington once described them as 'the greatest of all mountain explorers'.

When we finally started over to Rhamani, we met the ITBP team as they came down, looking tanned and mountain-drunk; their leader told me that they had spent two months up around the Sanctuary, right through the monsoon, 'through hurricanes, snow and all conditions'. It had taken them a month and five days to get to the Sanctuary itself – they described our progress as 'express' by comparison, helped by their path-clearing. Eight of them had reached the summit at 16.30 on 29 September and had stayed there twenty minutes to make a *puja*. He said nothing about their companion who had been killed by a stonefall on the mountain.

John Shipton was just ahead of me and had an unfortunate encounter with the ITBP wireless operator at a point where the path narrowed to a ledge beside the river. The ITBP operator was walking down towards us, his radio perched on his shoulder, playing *bhangra* music. John, passing him with his usual rapid shuffling gait, managed to accidentally jog the radio and sent it spinning down into the gorge below. The sound of tinny *bhangra* music was abruptly cut off as the radio smashed against the rock.

In the silence that followed, the wireless operator naturally lost his temper. He was a big Sikh, who dwarfed John. Neither of us could understand what he was saying, but it was clear that it was not complimentary. Fortunately Bimal, our Forestry Liaison Officer, came up behind us and cut the Sikh off in mid-flow: 'In some ways it's quite lucky that happened, you see. Because the regulations state quite clearly that under no circumstances can wirelesses be used in the National Park without the permission of the relevant official. And I am the relevant official. And you are not having the permission. So you see, in some ways it is quite lucky that you no longer have the wireless. Otherwise it would have been my duty to report you.' Bimal smiled his polite smile at the Sikh. It was a match-winning performance.

The rest of the group had spread out behind us, as by now it was wont to do, each member taking things at their own pace. I could see Jeff Ford and Barry Bond in the distance with George Band, planning their next trip, a proposed circumnavigation of Kangchenjunga; beyond them were 'the two Davids' as we called them, David Baber and David Sayer, who had been on Everest together; just behind was Gerry Becker, a loner who always kept very quiet; Natalena, by contrast a great talker, was with Mac and Loreto right at the back, although I could hear Mac even from this distance – having Mac in the Himalaya was a bit like having Colonel Hati from *The Jungle Book* leading his troupe.

We crossed over the Trisul Nala, a tributary gorge to the Rishi Ganges that peeled away south, and ate a picnic together just beyond by some small red rhododendrons. Sula had made us *masala dosas*, which Mac eyed cautiously, but which I tore into with relish. 'How come you've got half my stomach and twice my appetite?' he demanded.

Beyond, we passed through beautiful stands of birch forests, with rich, New England colours – ochres, reds and yellows, with the virgin bark of the birches showing through the peeling strips. I loitered to take photographs and let the others pass. Finally starting up the path again, I heard a flute playing ahead and rounded a corner to find

Puran Kudkha, one of the porters, lying on the grass with a younger boy listening entranced. Puran was playing a song about Nanda Devi, in which the singer tells his beloved that she is as beautiful as the mountain.

I listened for a while. 'Bull' Kumar came slowly up the path behind us and stopped, equally surprised by the scene. Then he broke into a little caper and danced slowly round to the music, to the delight of the porters.

Leaving the sunlit slopes behind, I rounded a bend in the river to come to Rhamani, and my world changed.

*

Rhamani is a fearful place.

It lies almost permanently in the shadow of the great cliffs that the Rishi Ganges throws up to each side as you approach the Sanctuary. The river narrows at Rhamani and there are few places to put up a tent. Our porters slept in dank caves at the bottom of the cliff walls, under great overhangs. Previous expeditions had carved their names on the cave walls; I saw a 'Dewan' dating back to 1936 and remembered the old man I had talked to back at Lata.

What with the ITBP's recent visit and our own influx of porters, there was dirt and litter everywhere in the narrow space. If you walked either side of the camp, you immediately came across piles of excrement.

From here we could see the terrifying box canyon up ahead, which guarded the Sanctuary. I could immediately see why even Shipton and Tilman had paused at the sight. I remembered Shipton's hair-raising description of clinging to ledges that petered out with 3,000-foot drops below.

The next day would see us having to negotiate this. John Shipton had already been ahead with Deva to rec-onnoitre the route. When he got back to Rhamani, excited and wild-eyed, he told us: 'It's the best and most fright-ening thing I've ever done in my life – total exposure. I thought I was going to die several times.'

Not all the party looked as delighted as John at this news. Many were already tired after what had been a tough and exhausting trek this far in the first place. The thought that only here did it begin to get both dangerous and extreme was too much.

The problem was that the exposure was so extended – it would take a full day of crawling along ledges and climbing narrow chimneys to reach the Sanctuary – and all this would be played out high up on the cliffside, with 3,000 feet of exposure below.

The mood was tense that night in the camp. Mac had already been shouting at John for not helping him in his complicated travel arrangements (directly after this, he had to fly to a meeting of the International Moun-taineering and Climbing Federation). Now no one was talking much.

Mac broke the silence: 'Some of us think mountains are worth dying for.' This did not make me feel any better. Mac saw that I wasn't looking too cheerful and took me to one side for a word: 'Don't worry, you'll be fine if you've got mountaineering experience.'

I had no mountaineering experience whatsoever, only

what Steve had required: 'a good head for heights'. Nor was I reassured by his next comment to the group: 'Look, this is just a game, we're all players and we can decide at any stage whether to withdraw or not.'

Others were looking concerned. Five of the seventeen announced that they would go no further.

That night I experienced real fear. The smell of the juniper wood that the porters were burning, mixed with the acrid burn-off from the paraffin stoves, began to make me nauseous. My tent was right by the river and the clouds had come in during the evening. The mist intensified the camp's claustrophobia and amplified the sound of people moving around me as they stumbled to the makeshift latrine; above all, it amplified the sound of the Rishi Ganges river, which was torrential at this point in the ravine. As I lay restlessly on my thin mattress on a jumble of rocks, the river seemed to be splitting and running either side of my brain. I found it impossible to sleep.

I became both disorientated and paranoid. I believed that with no mountaineering experience I could risk a serious accident on the gorge, or cause someone else a serious accident.

My tent closed in around me. After the lengthy trek, all pretence at organisation had long since passed and I was lying with my possessions piled around me. It felt as if all my emotions had spilt out with them, like the tent of Tracey Emin's in which she had pinned up the names of all those she had ever slept with.

I remembered Bill Aitken's words, that 'to reach the

Sanctuary one must believe in something that endures', and wondered what that was for me. Like the hero of the country song who has to choose whether to reach for the Gideon bible or the bottle on his bedside, I had two resources: my books or the Absolut Vodka miniatures. With uncharacteristic strength of mind, I passed on the vodka.

I had three books with me in the tent. One was Shipton's *Nanda Devi*, with his account of the gorge. Another was *The White Spider*, Heinrich Harrer's list of the many climbers who had died climbing the Eiger. And the last was *Paradise Lost*. None of them made for exactly restorative reading.

Using my head-torch, I tried reading Milton:

> horror and doubt distract
> His troubl'd thoughts, and from the bottom stirr
> The Hell within him, for within him Hell
> He brings, and round about him, nor from Hell
> One step no more than from himself can fly
> By change of place.

For some reason I kept thinking of Milton's blindness, perhaps because I was using the flickering head-torch. And I thought of the power of his imagination, writing without the cumbersome need to make an actual journey. What the hell was I doing here? I could at this moment be reading quietly about the horrors of the gorge in the safety of an armchair, with my children asleep by the light of the night nursery. And I thought of them, and the way that their heads would be lying on the pillow. It was unbearable. And then I remembered George's comment, about how I had looked like Mallory's corpse as I slept.

> Which way I flie is Hell; myself am Hell;
> And in the lowest deep a lower deep
> Still threat'ning to devour me opens wide,
> To which the Hell I suffer seems a Heav'n.

*

The next morning I awoke early. I tried to get a grip by repacking. From the recesses of my black bag I drew out a climbing harness and some carabiners.

I'd spent a restless night, with febrile dreams and imaginings: my body found on a slope, head down like Mallory's, the finders only interested in whether the camera beside me had any film. This blurred into the continued worry about whether I should be travelling with my film stock and diaries, or risk a porter rolling them over the edge. I remembered an argument I'd had with my wife before leaving. Then I worried about life insurance, which I didn't have. For once, it was a relief to be thinking about packing.

John appeared at the tent-flap with a choice of cereal bar to take for our lunch later, as he did each day – his discreet way of touching base with everyone. He was mumbling a bit and looking sheepish, as he often did after having been on a high the night before.

'Don't worry, it will be fine.'

I wanted to believe him. Still, it was a subdued break-fast. Bull was leaving us here. On saying goodbye, he gave each of the twelve remaining members of the expedition a red *bindi* mark on their foreheads. We watched the five others return down the valley.

Then we set off. I concentrated on following George Band's reassuringly large size-twelve boots up the mountain, which, as the slope straight out of camp was steep, always appeared to be directly in front of me. Once up the hill, we contoured around and found ourselves crawling high along the gorge itself.

The route was so extraordinary that now, when I look back, it hardly seems possible, a fantastical version of a Disneyland roller-coaster walk, but without the safety net. The way (for it was not a 'path') switchbacked up and down, over and around the huge buttresses. One moment you could be traversing around a cliff face on a ledge a foot wide, the next climbing up stone slabs to reach the next crossing-place. And just when the path narrowed to nothing, a chimney would take you up or down to the fragile beginnings of another track.

Our struggle to negotiate this was played out with the noise of the river seemingly roaring for blood below; across the gorge, the equally sheer cliffs of the northern side stared at us blankly, an unfortunate reminder of what we ourselves were climbing along.

Once we got close to the difficult sections, Jeff and Barry reminded me of some basic mountaineering disciplines, some of which came back as a residual memory from messing around on climbing walls years before. 'You've picked a great place to learn, Hugh,' said Jeff jocularly, as we gazed ahead at a sheer cliff.

'Yes,' I said, trying to sound equally relaxed and jocular. 'Uh, where's the route?' Jeff pointed to a thin wisp of a line that seemed to trace across the cliff face and then petered out. 'What happens when we get to that point?'

'We climb up,' said Jeff, and headed off at a brisk pace before I had time to think about this too much.

However, as the day wore on, my worries of the night before dispersed and I managed to find in myself that sense of detachment that Bull had once talked to me about. The fact that for hours we had the total exposure of a 3,000-foot drop beneath us as we made our way like flies along the side of the canyon walls became unreal. By focussing on the procedure for managing the fixed ropes and climbing the chimneys and slabs, I could ignore the vertiginous drops and overhangs.

Albert Chapman also cheered me up. He was the doughty President of the Yorkshire Ramblers Club, a group that sounds like a Sunday-afternoon institution but is the second-oldest climbers' association in Britain, after the Alpine Club. It has sent many climbers into the Himalaya. Like many Yorkshire institutions, the Ramblers were fond of their reputation for plain speaking, toughness and humour, and Albert was a suitably eccentric President. For today's climb he was wearing a fetching pair of bright orange paisley trousers and a floppy hat. At one point, he turned to me as I was struggling on a difficult section over some slabs: 'Did you know, Hugh, that if you heat up a George Formby record, it makes a lovely fruitbowl?' By the time I had finished laughing, I was on the other side.

A little further on, Albert had a nasty slip going round a fixed-rope section and fell. His carabiner held and he was left dangling over a 3,000-foot drop. With some difficulty, for Albert was not small, a nearby *sirdar* managed to pull the understandably shaken Yorkshireman back up to safety.

Even the most experienced mountaineers were looking chastened, for this was a dangerous cross between a true out-and-out rock climb and a trek, a 'scramble' to use a euphemism that belied the lack of protection afforded by a true climb. The Matterhorn is so dangerous and claims so many lives for similar reasons, because it can theoretically be ascended by those with relatively little experience, even though the quality of the rock is bad in places. Edward Whymper, who used the same euphemism to describe his first ascent of it in *Scrambles in the Alps*, took with him the young Douglas Hadow, who had no experience to speak of and who died on the descent, falling 3,000 feet to the Matterhorngletscher below.

It took about five hours of this 'scrambling' to get to Bhojgara, a place with distinctive circular stone slabs. We rested here with the porters. As they had never seen the gorge before, there was much discussion between them on the same issue that had occurred to me: that if this was what it was like under good conditions, what would our return descent be like if there was any snow and ice? It didn't bear thinking about. Some of the porters who huddled under a ledge looked particularly miserable. They would have to return this way twice, in order to keep us resupplied once we reached the Sanctuary.

Shipton's and Tilman's achievement in finding their way through here in the first place was extraordinary. By this stage in their exploration, they had been abandoned by all their porters, who had found the going too hard; only the three Sherpas were left to help them. Between the five of them, they were carrying the considerable supplies that they would need for serious exploration of the Sanctuary, as they threaded their way along the same precipitous ledges that we had been following. The Sherpas often removed their boots completely to improve their grip on the slippery rock.

The small team was continually coming to a dead end, as they tried to find 'escape routes' when each ledge ended. Shipton had a vivid description of the problem: 'We tried places which were quite obviously ridiculous; just as one searches under the teapot or in the coal-scuttle for a lost fountain pen when one has exhausted every likely place.'

As the way was so difficult to find, they were continually having to make hazardous river crossings to the other side of the Rishi Ganges, both to look ahead and to try to avoid the daunting buttress they nicknamed 'Pisgah', which blocked the way ahead to the Sanctuary on the southern side.

I could see why they were so alarmed by it. Pisgah seemed an impregnable obstacle, bulging out from the rock face with what looked like impossible overhangs and descending right down to the river below. But it was still some way in the distance and I had more immediate worries.

There were two formidable ascents directly ahead of us, each a steep 1,000 feet, before the business of traversing around tiny ledges began again. Then we came to a chimney, the 'vile-looking gully' that Shipton had surveyed from the other, northern side of the gorge and pronounced 'unpassable'.

When I talked later to others in the party, many agreed with me that by this stage the journey began to blur into an other-worldly experience, as difficult section followed difficult section along a route that seemed geometrically impossible to achieve, like an Escher drawing. Only by focussing intensely on each footstep could one maintain any rhythm or balance, and so the overall 'shape' of the journey in our memories quickly became indistinct.

The gorge itself had much to do with this. Shipton had reported: 'I found myself to be nervous and shaky on the steep slopes and slabs on which we had to climb. This was due to the fact that I was not yet used to the immense scale of the gorge and its surroundings. Tilman suffered from the same complaint.'

On the 'vile-looking gully', we had the advantage of fixed ropes and what Shipton called, dryly, 'the complete lack of any alternative', always a major incentive to get over a difficult section of rock. However, once above the chimney and momentarily congratulating myself, I was brought up short. For we had now reached the bottom of Pisgah. Above me was a wall of rock 1,000 feet high.

It was four o'clock in the afternoon, and we had spent nine hours of tortuous ascent and descent to get this far.

Altitude and continual exposure to a mile's fall below had exhausted many of the party, including me. The sight of the Pisgah wall was like a kick in the face. Shipton and Tilman had tried to cross the river again here to avoid it. When that had proved equally difficult, Tilman and Angtharkay had come back across the river, ascended beside the Pisgah buttress and eventually found a way through, while Shipton watched them from the other side, convinced it was impossible: 'The last frail link in that extraordinary chain of rock faults, which had made it possible to make our way along the grim precipices of the gorge, had been discovered.'

I found I needed to reach deep to carry on. With the childishness that altitude and hypoxic exhaustion bring on, I found the competitive pleasure of being one of the front runners of the group helped me. Way above, I finally got close to the narrow couloir that ascended up Pisgah, which Shipton had described as the last barrier to the 'Promised Land' beyond.

By now we were all tired. The couloir was a narrow ascent to a cairn right at the top, traditionally known as 'the Stairway to Heaven' because, as one porter told me, 'It doesn't matter whether you climb it and reach the Sanctuary or whether you fall off; you will reach heaven either way.'

Probably out of nervous hysteria at having got this far, I couldn't help humming the first few bars of the Led Zeppelin classic as I hauled myself up. Steve Berry overheard me. An old seventies dopehead in his youth, he countered: 'What are those lines from that Hendrix song – "There must be some way out of here, said the joker to the thief." '

In fact they were Bob Dylan's lines, sung by Hendrix, but I sensed it wasn't the moment to be pedantic with Steve. He again had his head down and was concentrating intently on the climb. Afterwards he told me that he'd 'felt like a horse before an impossible fence. My first emotion was to rebel against going up there – it was too frightening, too difficult altogether.'

But there was a way, a final, unexpected slip of the knot that released the noose: a ledge that led us off at an unexpected, oblique angle, followed by a steep climb. By this stage adrenaline had taken over and I was past caring what was below or above me, 'Stairway to Heaven' or not. Somehow I seemed to keep going and finally Steve and I were out of the gorge and the world opened up before us. We were looking at the Sanctuary.

I felt like a chimney sweep who, at last emerging from the narrow confines of a flue, suddenly sees the rooftops of London laid out before him. To the north, a great range of glaciers and moraine led to the curtain wall of the Inner Sanctuary. To the south, another great swathe of grassland swept around below Trisul. And to the east, dead in front of us and lit up by the last sun, was the imposing monolith of Nanda Devi herself, now revealed in 'awful majesty'.

The goddess showed off her many colours that night, as we camped near by at the site called Patalkhan, which Shipton and Tilman had also used. The cloud that was drifting into the Sanctuary valley somehow stayed off the mountain-face as it turned from pale gold to pink to a steely blue. Up close, we could see that the ramparts of the West Face were so steep and overhung that only a light coating of snow could cling to the few ledges and sheer inward-sloping walls. Steve Berry and I watched the light change on Nanda Devi with awe. We had arrived.

*

It would be difficult to give an adequate description of the loveliness of the country in which we found ourselves. Beauty of the wild, riotous kind such as one usually finds in high mountain regions we had expected; but we found, as well, luxuriant pasture, brilliant with wild flowers, and lakes, on whose deep blue and green surfaces was reflected the crusts of icy peaks; birds of great variety and brilliant colours, and large herds of *thar* and *bharal*, which were so tame and regarded these strange new visitors with such curiosity, that I was almost glad we had not brought a rifle. (Eric Shipton, 'The Inviolate Sanctuary of the Blessed Goddess', *Illustrated London News*, 12 January 1935)

For some reason, I had always imagined the Inner Sanctuary as being small and intimate, a mountain knot-garden. But in reality it was more like a veldt of wide grasslands, curling around the mountain in a way that managed to be both inviting and grandiose at one and the same time.

These grasslands were high above the tree-line, so there were few flowers but rather clean open expanses, great swathes of green sweeping south and east against the white of the glaciers and the skyline of fabulous peaks.

Some of the porters told me, with lust in their voices, that it was the best pasturage for goats that they had ever seen.

For Eric Shipton, the thrill of being at long last in totally unknown territory was unsurpassable: 'each corner held some thrilling secret to be revealed for the trouble of looking'. Tilman and he took a childlike pleasure in exploring their new world – they roamed the northern glaciers, transfixed by the great wall that connects Nanda Devi East to the main summit and attempting (and failing) various minor peaks around the Sanctuary.

That day of first arrival in 1934 must always have been a high point of Shipton's life. At just twenty-six he had, with Tilman, cracked the great Himalayan enigma of Nanda Devi and knew that he could now explore the Sanctuary's infinite possibilities.

Below our camp was the junction of the two rivers that joined to form the Rishi Ganges; one headed to the northern half of the Sanctuary. This was the direction that Shipton and Tilman took on their first entrance. When they came back later in 1934, after the monsoon, they explored the southern half. It was this route again that Tilman's 1936 expedition took with their Mana porters when they finally made the ascent of Nanda Devi, and we now followed them.

At the very start of this walk we had to negotiate a set of stone slabs where Tilman had memorably described the 'sahibs' getting stuck:

It was not a prepossessing place to look at . . . Each man took the line that seemed good to him, but all got into difficulties, and then was seen the comic sight of seven Sahibs strung out over the slabs in varying attitudes, all betraying uneasiness, and quite unable to advance. The Mana men, having savoured the spectacle to the full and allowed time for the indignity of the situation to sink in, came laughing across the slabs to our aid and led us gently over by the hand like so many children.

They were the worst sort of obstacle because they looked so much easier than they were. The steep stone slope below would act like a chute for anyone who slipped — and they were in full view of the camp. We had to tackle them immediately after breakfast, never a good moment. After only a few steps Alan Tate froze and found it difficult to continue, but was guided on by Jeff and Barry from behind. I found the very last step difficult and went flat on my buttocks, close enough luckily to the secure earth slopes to grab onto a handful of shrub, but hardly dignified.

Aside from a boulder field, which we then had tiresomely to pick our way through, ahead lay some agreeable walking over meadowland and moor to reach the camp at the very centre of the Sanctuary. I felt terrific, with the sun on my back and, more importantly, the gorge behind me. My pace picked up and I felt as if I was striding across the Scottish Highlands, with Steve Berry beside me.

Steve seemed preoccupied and was walking with his head down. I knew that there had been tensions with John Shipton about how long we should stay in the Sanctuary;

because of the delays caused by the ITBP party we were running two days late. I asked him if anything was the matter. 'It's the Gerber convention,' he said, 'I just can't seem to get it right.' He was still playing his bridge hand from the night before.

But I suspected another reason. Most climbers have one mountain written on their heart. I knew that Steve's was Gangkar Punsum, the highest mountain in Bhutan. Steve had led one of the very first (and last) expeditions to attempt this peak in 1986. At almost 25,000 feet, it had been described by Chris Bonington at the time as 'the highest unclimbed mountain available to Western Mountaineers in the world'.

As with our current trip, securing permission for it had been as arduous as the climb. The perennially prickly Bhutanese were annoyed that the only previous team they had ever let in to attempt the peak had demanded their money back – on the grounds that they had been unable to find the mountain, let alone climb it.

I could understand why. Gangkar Punsum lies in the wild far north of Bhutan, above the ancestral heartland of Bumthang, a place I had visited myself for a great *tsechu*, the Buddhist festival that is held once a year. Bumthang felt like the edge of the world, so I could only imagine what it must have been like for Steve, leading a large party of twenty-two to even more remote territory and to a mountain only ever seen by a few yak-herders.

The expedition was fraught with other problems. Doug Scott, the first British climber to summit Everest and a man with firm views, had publicly withdrawn from the team after arguing with Steve; the Bhutanese had asked for a hefty climbing fee of £30,000, while for every additional day that the team stayed in the country, the Bhutanese made it clear that there would be an extra penalty fee; Steve also had a film crew in tow, which, as I knew all too well, was not easy and could lead to conflicts of interest.

For Steve this was by far the most ambitious project he had ever been involved in. Most of his team were climbing friends from Bristol, who had been used to a loose-knit atmosphere of dope-smoking and hanging out together – indeed, going out together, as there were several female climbers on the expedition and a complicated web of relationships. Steve told me one story of how a group of them had woken up one day in Bristol with a hangover; feeling bored they had decided, on a whim, to hitch up to the Old Man of Hoy at the other end of the country, a climb of fearsome repute, and 'knock it off'.

In 1986 they were attempting to find a route up a mountain in the middle of nowhere, and, moreover, in the narrow window between the monsoon and winter.

In the end it was the weather that beat them. After a difficult climb, they had been forced to withdraw before reaching the summit of Gangkar Punsum by the early onset of winter, which was accompanied by ferocious gales. Steve had his tent destroyed around him one night as he slept at 20,500 feet, their Camp I. Then they had more problems with the Bhutanese authorities, who insisted on sending an Indian Army helicopter to evacuate them. Steve had been left with the bill – and the Bhutanese had refused to let anyone back to attempt Gangkar Punsum again. It remains unclimbed.

Steve had been the last to be evacuated. As the helicopter left, he looked at the mountain for the last time; in his words, 'living with her had been so intense that my own future had been forgotten. Now the practical implications of life were rushing towards me again and her beauty was perhaps a closed chapter in my life.'

Having been defeated once by the early onset of winter, Steve was now very conscious of it again and I noticed him glancing up at the clear sky with the thin streams of cloud that were beginning to curl into the Sanctuary. If the weather changed suddenly, we could easily be trapped. He did not want a repeat of Gangkar Punsum.

Steve's Bhutanese experience had left him with an abiding fascination with Buddhism and a thoughtful, controlled approach to life, qualities that I suspected might be tested in the next few days.

For there had now been time for the stress lines to emerge in the composition of the group. The dynamics of the expedition were complicated in any case. Steve Berry had organised it all and as Managing Director of Himalayan Kingdoms he was ultimately responsible for our safety. But the nominal leaders of the expedition were 'Bull' Kumar, who was providing all the Indian logistics, and John Shipton, a man who hated organisation with all the passion that only a sixties counter-culture rebel can manage. Meanwhile Mac was there as the representative of the International Mountaineering and Climbing Federation, and was part of the mountaineering establishment – all things that were anathema to John.

Effectively four people were holding onto the sheet, and the rest of us could get tossed in the middle. I liked them all as individuals, but I also sensed, in the words of Bette Davis, that we could be in for a bumpy ride.

That night there was another argument as we ate. John, who was feeling ill and had drunk a couple of large whiskies, railed against the self-glorification of so many mountaineers, who did it for the fame and prestige.

'What about the people who just go off and climb for the sheer pleasure of it?' he complained. 'There must be people out there who do incredible things' (he paused for effect) '*incredible* things, that no one ever knows about. I hate all those people who just want to write about their achievements.' He lapsed into silence. Unlike his father, John had never published an account of his considerable adventures.

Mac told a story about a man attempting all the 8,000-metre peaks by 'piggybacking' other expeditions, that is, joining them for an additional fee when they had already set up all the logistics. 'What's the point, when Reinhold Messner has already done them all – without oxygen! It's mountaineering by numbers.

'Of course,' he added, 'there is a real reason why people all over the world are drawn to mountains. They are the source of all water, and of all life.'

We all fell silent at this for a while. Then George began to tell a story, a story that had been hanging over the expedition but which I had never heard in full: the story of Willi Unsoeld and his daughter, Nanda Devi Unsoeld, who had died here, on the mountain, in a terrible expedition in 1976.

*

The expedition had started as a way of commemorating Tilman's ascent of 1936, forty years before. One of the climbers, the veteran Ad Carter, had even been on that first climb. Willi Unsoeld, their leader, had intended it as a spiritual as well as a mountaineering journey.

Unsoeld had been so taken by Nanda Devi on a previous visit to the region that he had named his daughter after the mountain and brought her with him when he returned in 1976. By then Nanda Devi Unsoeld (usually just called Devi) was twenty-two and, in the words of her obituary, 'young, blonde and beautiful'. She had always wanted to travel to the mountain, not simply because it was her namesake but because she shared her father's attraction to the idea of a Hindu sanctuary, a special and holy place. It had been hoped that she would be part of the group who reached the summit.

However, the expedition was quickly riven by internal bickering, which made the tragedy of Devi's later death even more bitter. In a way, these divisions highlighted what had happened to mountaineering since Unsoeld's great Everest climb in 1963, which had made him famous.

Willi Unsoeld's achievements on Everest had been sublime. He had done what many had considered to be impossible. Together with his climbing partner, Tom

Hornbein, he had led a new route up the West Ridge of Everest and then traversed across the summit to descend by a different route, the South Col.

Traverses were a mountaineering finesse that people played with on lesser peaks, where one could afford to have fun, like walkers who prefer a circular route to take in different scenery – not on Everest. The only traverse of such a scale that had ever been attempted before in the Himalaya had been on Nanda Devi in 1951, when the two lead French climbers had died.

Unsoeld and Hornbein pulled it off and returned to a heroes' welcome from President Kennedy and the mountaineering world, although at some cost. Unsoeld lost nine of his toes, was hospitalised for many months and claimed later that the experience had permanently damaged his 'mental acuity'.

That expedition had likewise had its disputes – what expedition doesn't? In particular there had been a division between those who favoured the fail-safe placing of the first American on the summit by the South Col route, and those, like Unsoeld, who wanted to try the more daring new West Ridge ascent and the traverse. But the expedition was made up of sober and rational men, many of them doctors or academics, and they worked through their differences with the most sensational of resolutions: they ended up doing both. When Unsoeld and Hornbein made their ascent, they had been preceded by two teams who had already climbed to the summit via the more established South Col route. It was a team of equals.

By the 1970s, such a collegiate atmosphere was becom-

top: Mount Hanuman by moonlight. *'That night I dreamt of the Tounot, the first mountain I climbed as a boy.'*

above: Porters around the fire at Dibrugheta.

OPPOSITE
'Rhamani is a fearful place: it lies almost permanently in the shadow of the great cliffs that the Rishi Ganges throws up to each side as you approach the Sanctuary.'

THIS PAGE
The Rishi Ganges gorge: 'As long as you've got a good head for heights, you'll be fine,' said Steve Berry.

Eric Shipton wrote that he could not 'get used to the immense scale of the gorge and its surroundings'.

The last section of the ascent to the
Sanctuary, described by the porters as
'The Stairway to Heaven'. *'Finally we
were out of the Gorge and the world
opened up before us. We were looking at
the Sanctuary.'*

Shaving in the Sanctuary.

Ian McNaught-Davis ('Mac'): *'Some of
us think mountains are worth dying for.'*

Hugh Thomson, with the lower
gorge behind.

The northern side of the Nanda Devi Sanctuary.

The southern side of the Sanctuary, with Mount Nanda Devi to the left.

The summit of Nanda Devi at sunset.

The memorial stone for Nanda Devi Unsoeld at the base of the mountain.

NEXT PAGE
The expedition camp below the West Face of Nanda Devi.

ing a thing of the past. Only suckers didn't get to the top – and if you were climbing Kangchenjunga, you certainly didn't stop short of the summit out of respect for local feeling. On Unsoeld's expedition to Nanda Devi in 1976, there was a strong feeling that an elite group of lead climbers were using the others as 'mules' to carry supplies to a final camp, so that the elite could stand on their shoulders for the final ascent.

The idea of 'lead climbers' was nothing new – but the process by which they emerged had previously been more democratic, more a process of seeing who did well on the approach and was in good shape (as Hillary and Tenzing had shown on Everest in 1953 when they impressed the others by their load-carrying teamwork). Here right from the beginning there was a 'fast-track' team, led by the egotistical John Roskelley, who continually pressured those, like Devi, whom they felt were not up to their level of fitness. Unsoeld was already bewildered by this before his daughter started to feel ill. Ad Carter, used to the gentility of a previous generation, was so upset by the constant arguments that he turned back.

Part of the problem was class, which, in the States just as much as in Britain, was supposed to melt away in the democracy of the mountains but remained stubbornly insoluble. John Roskelley had blue-collar roots and at one time had been a construction worker, while Willi Unsoeld and Ad Carter were from a more patrician, academic background. Unsoeld had been to theological college, and had a strong spiritual bent, inspired partly by his early experiences in the Himalaya, which Roskelley did not share.

Roskelley climbed purely to get to the top at all costs; Unsoeld and Carter for the experience.

Roskelley, who afterwards produced what is widely considered one of the most bad-tempered and ungenerous accounts of an expedition ever written, described Devi Unsoeld as not being a good climber. This was far from the case. Others said that she was accomplished and impressive, particularly on snow and ice. She was certainly a tough, independent woman, who had twice taken the overland route to Asia. And unlike Roskelley, she had taken the time to learn Nepalese and showed a real empathy for Hindu theology and people.

Roskelley's book, *Nanda Devi: The Tragic Expedition*, marks a decisive change in tone from its literary predecessors; it is to mountaineering books what Coppola's *The Conversation* and Nicolas Roeg's movies were to film at around the same time. From the sunny uplands of the sixties, when the challenge was simple – 'There's the mountain, go climb it' – now the landscape is post-Altamont, post-Watergate, and is correspondingly dark and troubled. The belief in a community of like-minded souls has gone. The mood is egotistical, Nietzschean. If mountaineers allowed themselves to take drugs – and not for nothing was Valium called 'the climber's little friend' – by now they would all have moved on from dope to amphetamines.

Mountaineers distance themselves with a laugh from the Kangchenjunga expedition launched by Aleister Crowley at the turn of the century, with his brutal disassociation from any deaths that happened around him.

But how different was the new mountaineering ethos from his infamous credo: 'Do what thou wilt shall be the whole of the Law'?

Roskelley records the following conversation that he had with Elliot Fisher, another team member, when they were halfway up the mountain:

ROSKELLEY: This mountain's dangerous and someone's going to be killed.

FISHER: If that's what you believe, then why don't you leave and get off the mountain?

ROSKELLEY: Because it's not going to be me.

It wasn't him. Roskelley had summited with the other two 'elite climbers' and was back at advance base camp when Devi Unsoeld, just below the top and about to make her own summit attempt, died from medical complications brought on by a hernia and some still-undiagnosed altitude condition. She was with her father and the young climber Andy Harvard, to whom she had become engaged while on the mountain.

As the tragedy had happened at 24,000 feet, it was impossible to bring her body back down. Willi Unsoeld and Harvard bundled Devi up in her sleeping bag and slipped her over the precipice of the North-East Face, as if, in Willi's distraught words, 'committing her to the deep'.

Roskelley's book, and many subsequent ones, have since picked the mountaineering elements of what he described as 'the tragic expedition' obsessively clean: the route taken; the arguments; who should have done what and when; the blame for Nanda Devi Unsoeld's death. 'Nanda Devi 1976' has joined the blacklist that mountaineers like to keep of what can go terribly wrong on a peak, along with 'Nanga Parbat 1934', 'K2 1939', 'K2 1986' and the Everest disasters of 1996. There is nothing that climbing literature likes so much as a good post-mortem.

But in the conflation of endless detail, these accounts overlook the simplest and most resonant element. Devi Unsoeld was a mountaineer who had everything going for her in her approach to the mountain: as well as the necessary technical skills, she empathised with the local people and was exemplary in the way she worked with her colleagues in the team, a rare quality that was thrown into highlight by the bad faith and temper of some around her; she was even named after Nanda Devi. She desperately wanted to reach what she felt was a spiritual beacon in a corrupt world. If anyone had the right attitude, it was her. And yet the mountain had taken her life. It is a terrible example of what can happen when the dream of a sanctuary, one of mankind's most powerful mythopoeic enticements, collides with the reality of trying to reach it.

A memorial stone had been erected in the meadows of the south Sanctuary, not far from the camp, by Kiran Kumar, Bull's brother, one of the Indian climbers with the American expedition. I had seen it that evening as I approached, silhouetted against the skyline. An extract from Devi Unsoeld's last diary was inscribed on the stone:

'I stand upon a wind-swept ridge at night with the stars bright above and I am no longer alone but I waver and merge with all the shadows that surround me. I am part of the whole and am content.'

*

Our camp was right in the heart of the Sanctuary, below the West Face of Nanda Devi. It was in a small bowl that curled down from the grasslands and seemed to funnel the winds blowing down from the glaciers.

It was bitterly cold that night, after George had finished his story about Nanda Devi Unsoeld. Even a dinner of vodka, mushroom soup and whisky didn't help. I was sharing a tent with Steve Berry; for a while I sat outside, listening to his hacking cough and drinking beguilingly sugared tea with the porters.

Like John Shipton and many others, Steve had the flu-like virus that seemed to be going around the group and was in a bad way. He had even stopped smoking his usual little *bidis*, Indian home-rolled cigarettes, which I was grateful for; while I always trusted a man who smoked in the mountains, I didn't normally want to share a tent with him.

Later that same night, he told me for the first time that his father, who had first inspired him to climb in Kashmir, was seriously ill with Alzheimer's – to the extent that Steve had wondered whether he should have come on the expedition at all. We were of course completely unable to get news of the outside world, and Steve was worried that his father might be deteriorating.

I felt very close to him. He had probably been the single person most responsible for getting us all to the Sanctuary.

The next morning, when I wandered out for ablutions and a first cup of tea, I saw a herd of 'blue sheep', *bharal*, on the ridge above us, examining us carefully and with some surprise.

Bharal are confused and confusing animals; although they look like sheep, they behave like goats. Nor are they blue. Their taxonomic name is *Pseudois nayaur*, *'pseudois'* meaning 'false sheep'. I looked at them through binoculars, their horns silhouetted against the white dawn light, as they stood warily on the skyline. They have much to be wary about, being the principal prey for snow leopards, of whom there were thought to be many in the Sanctuary, given the absence of humans.

Mac had to leave the Sanctuary early to get to his mountaineering conference in Europe. I was sorry to see him go, not least because as the expedition had worn on, he was the only person who could still be enthusiastic over breakfast.

Meanwhile John Shipton wanted to take a small party on to the old base camp in the south of the Sanctuary. It was from there that Tilman and his Anglo-American team had successfully first climbed the mountain in 1936, two years after he and Eric Shipton had solved the problem of getting into the Sanctuary. Eric had not been with his old friend for the summit attempt, as he had already begun the long series of reconnaissances of Everest that were to occupy him for so long, and bear so little fruit.

Indeed, his trip to Everest that season was so unsuccessful that Eric hurried over to the Garhwal, hoping to join up with Tilman. He arrived too late, after the peak had been climbed. As was to start becoming a pattern in his life, he was never quite in the right place at the right time. Instead Shipton joined a different team led by Henry Osmaston to survey the Sanctuary, work that Shipton always enjoyed. The surveying team included a young Sherpa called Tenzing Norgay, who impressed Shipton so much that he took him on subsequent Everest expeditions.

On hearing the news that Tilman and Noël Odell had climbed Nanda Devi, Shipton wrote to a friend: 'What a glorious effort of Bill & Odell to have climbed Nanda Devi. I am overjoyed that it was Bill who did the touchdown – he so thoroughly deserves every inch of his success ... I confess I wished I had been with them instead of wasting time on that ridiculous Everest business.'

After Tilman and Shipton had left the mountain in 1936, the Sanctuary fell silent for many years. First came the war, then the lure of Nepal when it finally opened its borders to the West, so until the 1950s no one disturbed the private world that the 'Terrible Twins', as they called themselves, had roamed so happily.

But it did not fall completely silent. For the Sanctuary received one bizarre and little-known visit a few months after the outbreak of the Second World War.

Just after Christmas Day 1939, a young pilot by the name of T.G. Waymouth was about to make a routine training flight across the Punjab plains from Ambala, a town north of Delhi where there was an RAF base. Waymouth needed the training because he had never done an extended flight before in his new aircraft, a twin-engine

Bristol Blenheim Mark I. Shortly before take-off he decided that the plains were too boring a route; as he put it, 'I wanted to fly over new country.'

Nothing came any newer than the summit of Nanda Devi, which had never been photographed from the air nor indeed been flown over. So, for no better reason than the fact that it was the highest mountain in the British Empire, plus, one suspects, a fair amount of Christmas lubrication, he decided to go there.

As he later admitted, this was not the most sensible of decisions. The Himalaya is a notoriously dangerous place to fly even in a modern aircraft. Waymouth and his crew were supposedly accustomising themselves to a new plane. They had light clothing suitable for a low flight over the scorching Indian plains ('We were inadequately dressed'). Nor, more seriously, did they have any oxygen with them, and as Nanda Devi is 25,640 feet high, flying over it would be unsafe. This was ironic, given that mountaineers had started using oxygen at similar altitudes precisely because of the experience of pilots. The only relevant piece of equipment with them was a camera, a folding 4.5 Zeiss Ikonta, with an excellent Zeiss lens.

It is unclear whether they told their commanding officer where they were going, but given the circumstances it seems highly unlikely. Waymouth took off, rose above the perpetual 'dust haze' that hovers at 8,000 feet over the Indian plain, and then started to gain real altitude as he approached Dehra Dun and the foothills of the Garhwal. He could see the peak of Nanda Devi ahead. As they got higher and closer, in Waymouth's terse words,

'The cold was intense and we had no oxygen.'

Undeterred, Waymouth made a great circuit of the Nanda Devi massif, starting over the southern glacier and crossing over the twin peaks of Nanda Devi to Shipton's 'Great North glacier', then wheeling over the Sanctuary and exiting via the 'huge razor-like ridge at over 21,000 feet', which runs down from Sunderdhunga Col. Judging from the resulting photos, and given their lack of oxygen, they could only do this by flying extremely close: 'The mountains brushed my wing-tips.' It was a clear winter's day, and the sunlight bouncing off the snow and glaciers was intensely bright.

The plane seemed absolutely silent as it coasted around something that no one has ever seen before or since: Nanda Devi and the Sanctuary in the depths of winter, under full snow.

Waymouth noticed the stark contrast between the open sunny slopes to the south of the mountain (the route that Tilman had ascended) and the forbidding northern side, where Nanda Devi Unsoeld was later to die.

Although Waymouth managed to keep going by taking deep breaths, his navigator was almost overcome by the lack of oxygen; they therefore decided to return as fast as they could to what was (reading between the lines of the subsequent report of this episode) what the Services call a 'God Almighty bollocking'.

Why did they do it? Was it some memory of *Lost Horizon*, James Hilton's phenomenally successful book of 1933 about a lost 'Shangri-La', which had been turned into a Hollywood movie and begins with just such a flight over the Himalaya? Or simply a case of too much brandy with the Christmas pudding?

After the war, and impressed by his audacity, Eric Shipton helped Waymouth write up his account of the flight. However, Shipton couldn't help pointing out that they had got their mountains wrong, mistaking Nanda Ghunti for Trisul, probably because they had used too small-scale a map – 1:1,000,000, designed for long-range work, not close-quarter reconnaissance. Given his antipathy for the military mindset, one can imagine that he enjoyed pointing out the RAF's blunders. And he had, after all, been forced to walk in himself.

*

Eric Shipton's problem with the military mindset was to surface more seriously a few years later, when he was replaced as leader on the 1953 Everest expedition precisely for lacking the military qualities that John Hunt was thought to have.

Yet despite the fact that Hunt's subsequent ascent of Everest was ostensibly a victory for all that Shipton most disliked – the large expedition, the siege mentality – he prophetically foresaw that it was actually its death knell because, once the highest peak in the world had been climbed, there was no military imperative left to climb any more. He wrote:

> The climbing of Mount Everest will, I believe, open a new era of mountaineering in the Himalayas. Mountaineers wishing to climb and explore in the Himalayas

will be forced to do so on their own initiative, and on modest resources. They will discover how incredibly small those resources can be, while still providing all their needs. Above all, they will find in the simplicity of their approach the true enjoyment of their endeavour.

A few large-scale expeditions did continue, particularly to Everest – the American expedition there in 1963 with its 900 porters, or Bonington's 1975 siege assault of the South-West Face – but in general the move has been towards a lighter alpinist style with small teams or, indeed, solo climbers, taking the approach that Shipton and Tilman had first advocated in their books on Nanda Devi.

Something of the enormous resilience and courage of Shipton can be seen from the way in which he recovered from his Everest disappointment in 1953. For in the next decade, the sixties, he was to open up a whole new area for mountaineering: Patagonia, then still a wilderness with, as Shipton wrote, 'the word "Inesplorado" written across it'.

Reading Shipton's accounts of this unexplored wilderness when I was at college made me want later to take my own expeditions to South America. And Shipton inspired a whole line of British adventurers who valued exploring the valleys and passes of the world more than the prestige of a first ascent: men like John Tyson, and the influential Scottish writer and mountaineer W.H. Murray, who at the end of his long life wrote that 'the richest Himalayan experience comes in exploratory travel and climbing, not the siege of a big peak'.

In some ways, reaching the Nanda Devi Sanctuary was the achievement truest to Eric Shipton's own personality. The fact that he never stood on the summit of the mountain does not matter; indeed, it is a testament in itself. Shipton was a wanderer in the best traditions of German romanticism, a Klingsor who enjoyed the highways and byways, but was not obsessed by the need to plant a flag on the top. If one looks at his long and illustrious mountaineering career (detailed in a fine memoir by his friend Peter Steele), there are surprisingly few peaks and many, many areas of previously untravelled country.

Already after his very first Everest expedition in 1933, he was writing: 'I had a mighty longing to detach myself from the big and cumbersome organisation which for some reason had been thought necessary for an attack on the more lofty summits of the earth.'

One senses that in later years Shipton was reluctantly forced into bigger and bigger 'organisations' at higher and higher altitudes, above all with his Everest expeditions, despite often admitting that he didn't enjoy them. This was partly to maintain his position as an explorer who could write and lecture on ever-increasing achievements.

In *Upon That Mountain* (1943) he comments mournfully: 'There are some, even among those who have themselves attempted to reach the summit, who nurse a secret hope that Mount Everest will never be climbed. I must confess to such feelings myself.'

And when traversing around the Sanctuary, he had at

one point 'begun to hope that we had proved the mountain [Nanda Devi] to be unclimbable'.

We ourselves were only allowed to reach the Sanctuary, not attempt the peak, which I knew some of our party would dearly like to have done. But leaving aside my own abilities to climb it anyway, I was content to have got this far and to contemplate the mountain at the centre of the Sanctuary, aware that it was unlikely I should ever be able to return.

*

My heart's in the highlands / at the break of dawn / by the beautiful lake of the black swan. / Big black clouds / like chariots that swing down low. / Well my heart's in the highlands / only place left to go.

Bob Dylan, 'Highlands'

I didn't want to join the small group that John Shipton was taking to the base camp at the southern end of the Sanctuary. It was Sunday and my heart rebelled at the thought of another day pounding a trail, let alone a forced march that would take ten hours there and back. We were, after all, now in the centre of the Sanctuary, so why go any further?

I wanted to roam the gullies and byways of this hidden world. Nothing quite heightens the senses like the knowledge that no one has ever seen what you are looking at. I have experienced it before with Inca ruins.

The Sanctuary, of course, was an unrivalled example of

high Himalaya pasture: lush grasslands, roamed by *thar* and snow leopards, ringed by profiles of mountains so storybook perfect that they could have been the cut-out for a Hollywood set (indeed, before he left us that morning Mac had tried to sing me a Julie Andrews number from *The Sound of Music*).

But what made it special was that it was a private place. Like a secret garden, or the dressing-room of a band, it was the access or rather the lack of it that made it both exciting and different.

Taking just Bishen with me, I headed up high towards Trisul, on the western side of the Sanctuary. We came across a large boulder that Bishen was sure, from the tracks and debris, had been slept under by a snow leopard. Lying back and eating a picnic lunch there in the sun, I could see the whole length of the Sanctuary from north to south, with glaciers at both ends; even the great western face of Nanda Devi was diminished by distance. The cloud was below me; the layers of glacial ice and cloud seemed to blur together in shades of white and grey. I thought of Swami Rama-Krishna's story of the seeker who climbs up the valley to the Sanctuary and then is forbidden by God to return to the world of men.

And I remembered again days as a boy in the Tounot basin; there had been the same sense of an enclosed world, albeit on a far lesser scale, and of time dropping off the rim of the earth. Shipton had written when in the Sanctuary: 'My most blissful dream as a child was to be in some such valley, free to wander where I liked.'

Now I felt totally relaxed, as if I'd just had a bath —

which was far from the case, as I hadn't washed for weeks. Mountaineers sometimes tell of out-of-body experiences, when they look down to see themselves at some moment of extremity or danger; this famously happened to Doug Scott on his first ascent of Everest. I felt quite the reverse: that in some curious way, my wandering shadow self, which had propelled me with a certain restlessness through life, had come home inside me and that there was nowhere left to go.

I buried my copy of *Paradise Lost* in a cairn high on the hill, as I had no intention of carrying it all the way back, and rested in a small glade that caught the sun, my head propped up on my pack. As I dozed in the heat, I thought of a moment on Mount Kilimanjaro when I had woken early during the ascent of the Western Breach, looked out of my tent and seen the mountain's own shadow stretching away in the dawn light across the panoply of clouds below. And as the sun came up higher I had seen what is called a 'brocken spectre' – my own shadow cast on the cloud in such a way that it seemed to sink into the cloud and become three-dimensional, embodied in mist. Occasionally mountains offer such moments of transcendence.

Later I wandered back to our camp in the happy knowledge that from now on it was all downhill, my tent was already up, Steve would be ready for some cards, and there was whisky to drink. Sula had even cooked some spicy potato fritters.

By that evening, John and his small group had returned from Tilman's old 1936 base camp after a long slogging day; Jeff had fallen in a boulder field and gashed his thigh badly, which needed dressing.

It was becoming clear that we could not stay in the Sanctuary much longer. The weather was changing and getting colder: the lowering jet-stream was beginning to tear great prayer-scarves of cloud off Nanda Devi's summit. Some incoming porters bore tales of rain and snow moving up with them from the valley as they brought fresh supplies. If we got cut off by snow, we would be in real trouble – Tilman had described a similar situation in the gorge as 'a nightmare'.

Before I had come, an Indian mountaineering friend, Yatish Bahaguna, had told me that this had happened to him thirty years before. His team had been trapped in the Inner Sanctuary for seven days because of snow. On the eighth day he told the porters, 'Either we die staying or we die moving.' A handful of the fittest managed to get down the gorge and on to Joshimath, a forced march that they completed in just three days. They sent back a helicopter for the others, who by then were at their limits of exposure and hunger.

Because our final permission to enter the Sanctuary had come so late, getting an additional radio-communications permit had proved impossible and so we had no means of summoning assistance. We likewise had only a few days' food with us (we had left supplies just below the gorge for our return journey). Akshay cheered us with the story of how five members of his uncle's expedition to Everest had been cut off in their tent by bad weather and had simply starved to death, his uncle having already died in a fall. Clearly we would need to get out the following day, probably by going all the way back to Rhamani in one forced march.

Like many summiteers, we had achieved our objective only to realise that we would, almost immediately, have to return. We would leave the Sanctuary tomorrow, although John Shipton and I would be departing 'with wandering steps and slow'. But for now, I could sit above the camp in the meadow, which was still catching the sun.

Directly across from me was the sheer West Face of Nanda Devi, all 10,000 feet of it still unclimbed, sometimes described as one of the last great challenges of modern mountaineering. Looking up, with the eagles circling high above, I felt I was staring at the walls of Mordor. Someone would undoubtedly die trying to climb it.

As I sat in the little meadow at the centre of the Sanctuary, beneath Nanda Devi's great ramparts, I thought of the Indian mountaineer who had recently been killed, and of Nanda Devi Unsoeld, twenty-two years old, whose memorial tablet was near by; all around it were memorials for others who had died here as well, many of them porters. I thought of all those mountaineers who had died in pursuit of what, at the end of it, is only an idea.

With the birds wheeling and circling around the serrated cliff edges above, and with the beauty of the meadow around me, I thought of all those pilgrims who had been drawn up into the mountains, and of those who had found what they were looking for – a 'belief in something that endures', to use the phrase with which Bill Aitken had first sent me here.

And I remembered an old *koan* of the Buddhists, the first to venerate Nanda Devi, which tells the story of an old sage instructing his pupils: 'When I was young,' he says, 'I believed that a mountain was just a mountain. Then, when I began the long process to *nirvana*, enlightenment, I realised that there was much more to a mountain and that it was a symbol of many other things. But now that I have achieved nirvana, I realise that a mountain is, indeed, just a mountain.'

CODA

Ian McNaught-Davis produced a report for the International Mountaineering and Climbing Federation, recommending that the Sanctuary be opened under strict controls for a few limited expeditions. A small official Indian team visited it in 2001 on behalf of the Indian Mountaineering Federation, and reported likewise.

At the time of writing, the Sanctuary is still closed and the Indian Government shows no desire to open it.

Personally I am only too happy if it remains closed. But then I've been there.

CHRONOLOGY

1817–20   Nanda Devi is surveyed by William Webb and John Hodgson. It is thought to be the highest mountain in the world until 1857, when Everest (Chomolungma) is 'discovered' by the West.

1830   The first British commissioner of Garhwal, G.W. Traill, crosses to the east of Nanda Devi over a pass that is later named after him.

1883   W.W. Graham enters the outer Nanda Devi Sanctuary from the west, via Lata, and gets as far as the Rishi Ganges gorge, but then turns back defeated.

1893   Kurt Boeck tries to enter the Sanctuary from the north-east.

1905   Tom Longstaff explores the south-eastern approaches to Nanda Devi, looks down from 'Longstaff Col' into the Inner Sanctuary, but is unable to descend.

1907   Longstaff returns to the Nanda Devi area with A.L. Mumm and Charles Bruce, after their request to attempt Everest is refused. They try to penetrate the Inner Sanctuary from the north but fail. Instead they reach the summit of nearby Trisul, at 23,360 feet the highest peak to be climbed until Kamet in 1931. Mumm uses oxygen on the ascent. From the top of Trisul they can again look down into the Inner Sanctuary.

1926   Hugh Ruttledge attempts to breach the Sanctuary

from the north-east, in an expedition with R.C. Wilson and Howard Somervell. He fails.

1927   Ruttledge and Longstaff fail in their attempt to enter the Sanctuary from the south-west.

1932   Ruttledge returns to Nanda Devi with an expedition. This time he attempts to enter from the south, but again fails.

Ruttledge writes an article in *The Times*, describing the difficulties of entering the Sanctuary.

1934   Eric Shipton and H.W. 'Bill' Tilman mount an expedition to the Sanctuary. They succeed in entering the Inner Sanctuary via the Rishi Ganges gorge, working closely with their three Sherpa companions, Angtharkay, Pasang and Kusang.

1936   Tilman returns to the Sanctuary with an Anglo-American expedition, which he co-leads with T. Graham Brown and Charles Houston. The summit of Nanda Devi is reached for the first time, by Noël Odell and Tilman.

1939   An unauthorised British flight is made over the summit of Nanda Devi by T.G. Waymouth.

1950   The first ascent of Annapurna is made by a French expedition. Herzog and Lachenal summit. Herzog is badly frost-bitten on the descent. As the first 8,000-metre peak to fall, this supplants Nanda Devi in the record books as the highest mountain ever climbed.

1951   A French expedition to Nanda Devi is led by Roger Duplat. Duplat and Gilbert Vignes die in the summit attempt. The expedition includes Tenzing Norgay, who searches for the lost climbers.

1953   A British expedition led by John Hunt makes the first ascent of Everest. Edmund Hillary and Tenzing Norgay summit. Charles Evans is the deputy leader and George Band the youngest member of the expedition.

1955   A British expedition led by Charles Evans makes the first ascent of Kangchenjunga. George Band and Joe Brown are the first to summit.

1960   India mounts an unsuccessful attempt on Everest.

1962   India mounts a second expedition to Everest, which also fails.

1963   On an American expedition to Everest, Tom Hornbein and Willi Unsoeld successfully complete the traverse from the West Ridge to the South Col.

1964   Narindar 'Bull' Kumar leads an Indian expedition to Nanda Devi, with a successful ascent.

1965   The first successful Indian ascent of Everest, led by Captain Mohan S. Kohli, with Narinder 'Bull' Kumar as his deputy.

1965–67   The CIA sponsors various secret expeditions to put nuclear-powered spying devices on top of Nanda Devi and Nanda Kot.

1970   A British expedition led by Chris Bonington climbs the south face of Annapurna. This initiates a new phase of Himalayan climbing, exploring routes up the faces of the 8,000-metre peaks rather than along their ridges.

1974   'Inner-Line' restrictions on the Sanctuary are lifted.

        An Anglo-Indian expedition led by Chris Bonington and Balwhant Sandhu makes the first ascent of Changabang.

1976   Yoshinori Hasegawa and Kazushige Takami successfully complete the first traverse between the east and main peaks of Nanda Devi. They are members of a twenty-one-strong Japanese expedition.

        Willi Unsoeld leads an American expedition to Nanda Devi to mark the fortieth anniversary of Tilman's and Odell's first successful ascent. His daughter, Nanda Devi Unsoeld, dies on the mountain.

The West Face of Changabang is climbed by Peter Boardman and Joe Tasker.

1977 Narinder 'Bull' Kumar leads an expedition to Kangchenjunga, making the first ascent from the Sikkimese side.

1978 'The Nanda Devi Caper' by Howard Kohn in the magazine *Outside*, publicises the story of a nuclear-powered generator lost in the Sanctuary by the CIA-sponsored missions.

Britons Terry King and Paul Lloyd make an attempt on the North Face of Nanda Devi. They are arrested on coming down by Border Police.

1981 Indian Army expedition to the Sanctuary, led by Kiran Kumar. Five members die.

1982 The Nanda Devi Sanctuary is closed by the Indian Government, ostensibly for ecological reasons.

1985 Indian expedition to Everest. Kiran Kumar dies, along with four of his colleagues.

1993 The Indian Government sends in a team of army sappers on an expedition to help 'clean up' the Sanctuary.

2000 An expedition led by Narinder 'Bull' Kumar and John Shipton is allowed to enter the Sanctuary to make a feasibility report on whether it should be reopened.

GLOSSARY

aarti	Hindu ritual marking dawn and dusk.
ata	Wholemeal flour used to make *chapattis*, flat Indian bread.
bhangra	Indian pop music.
bharal	*Pseudois nayaur*, known as 'blue sheep'.
bindi	A decorative mark placed on the forehead by Hindus to indicate the 'third' or 'spiritual' eye.
box canyon	A canyon whose sides rise perpendicularly from the waters, as does the Rishi Ganges gorge when leaving the Sanctuary.
carabiner	A ring with a spring clip, used in mountaineering to attach to a rope or harness.
chai	Indian tea.
col	The lowest part of a gap between two mountains.
couloir	A steep narrow gully.
dalits	The name by which the lowest caste of Hindusm, previously known as 'untouchables', prefer to be called. It means 'the oppressed'.
darshan	To have 'auspicious sight' of a deity.

Garhwal	A region of the Indian Himalaya, near the border with Tibet and Nepal.
IMF	Indian Mountaineering Federation.
ITBP	Indo-Tibetan Border Patrol.
jumar	A clamp for holding onto a rope.
karim	An Indian board game.
karma	The Hindu law of moral cause and effect: all one's actions will ultimately be made manifest, whether in this life or a subsequent one.
koan	A fable used by Buddhist masters to instruct their pupils, particularly in the Zen Buddhist tradition.
kharak	Summer grazing ground.
Kumaon	The neighbouring region to the Garhwal.
lakh	A unit of 100,000, usually used of rupees (as in 'a government minister was discovered to have hidden thirty *lakh* under his bed').
lammergeyer	The bearded vulture of the Himalaya, and the largest bird of prey found in Asia, with a ten-foot wingspan.
lingam	A phallic emblem, associated with the worship of Shiva.
maidan	A hide, used for hunting.
masala dosa	A *dosa* is a thin crêpe made from lentil and rice flour; *masala dosas* are stuffed with vegetable curry.
Padmasambhava	An eighth-century sage credited with bringing Buddhism from India to Tibet and Bhutan.
pakora	A deep-fried fritter, popular in India as a

	snack; often served by swimming pools.
pisaru	A Pakistani card game.
pradhan	The head man of a village.
puja	A ceremony involving an offering to a Hindu deity.
sadhu	A 'holy man'. There are a multitude of different sects, but the primary division is between those who follow Vishnu (the Vaishnavites) and those who follow Shiva (Shaivites). As the Garhwal is very much 'the land of Shiva', Shaivite *sadhus* and their more extreme representatives, the *naga sadhus*, tend to dominate.
sannyasi	A renunciant, who abjures family, business and the trappings of their previous existence to seek salvation.
Shaivite	A follower of Shiva.
Sherpas	A race of Tibetan origin who now live largely in Nepal, near Everest, and have provided some of the world's finest mountaineers.
Shiva	A Hindu god, often represented as the 'wild man' of the Hindu pantheon, who is considered to be both creator and destroyer.
sirdar	The leader of a group of porters.
stupa	A Buddhist burial mound or monument, usually circular.
terma	A sacred Buddhist text thought to have been buried in the Himalaya by sages such as Padmasambhava for future generations to find.
thar	A goat-like animal native to the Himalaya.
tsechu	An annual Buddhist festival.

Ushba   Mount Ushba, a peak in the Caucasus regarded as exceptionally beautiful.

Uttarakhand   The traditional name for the mountain area formed by the Garhwal and Kumaon. When the area seceded from Uttar Pradesh to become a separate state in 2000, it was called Uttaranchal, although there are moves to restore the traditional name.

Uttar Pradesh   Large Indian state extending north across the plains from Delhi. Until 2000 it included the Garhwal and Nanda Devi.

Vaishnavite   A follower of Vishnu.

Vishnu   Along with Shiva, one of the most important Hindu deities; the preserver of the natural order.

yatra   A pilgrimage trail.

The heights of mountains have been given in feet throughout, except when referring to the '8,000-metre peaks', a special category for the fourteen Himalayan mountains over that altitude (26,240 ft).

SELECT BIBLIOGRAPHY

Place of publication is London, unless stated otherwise.

Aitken, Bill, *The Nanda Devi Affair* (Penguin India, 1994)

Aitken, Bill, 'Shepherd of Nanda Devi Sanctuary', in *Himalayan Journal*, vol. 38, 1980–1

Allen, Charles, *The Search for Shangri-La: A Journey into Tibetan History* (Little, Brown, 1999)

Aris, Michael, *Hidden Treasures and Secret Lives* (Kegan Paul International, 1989)

Berry, Steven, *The Thunder Dragon Kingdom* (Crowood Press, 1988)

Berry, Steven, 'Permit Me, Sanctuary', in *Himalayan Journal*, vol. 58, 2002

Boardman, Peter, *The Shining Mountain* (Hodder & Stoughton, 1978)

Bonington, Chris, *The Everest Years* (Hodder & Stoughton, 1986)

Brown, Hamish, 'Nanda Devi Sanctuary', in *Mountain*, vol. 61, 1978

Brown, Joe, *The Hard Years* (Victor Gollancz, 1967)

Corbett, Jim, *The Man-Eating Leopard of Rudraprayag* (London, 1947)

Curran, Jim, *High Achiever: The Life and Climbs of Chris Bonington* (Constable, 1999)

Dang, Hari, 'Three Mountains – and Nanda Devi', in *Himalayan Journal*, vol. 25, 1964

Evans, Charles and Band, George, 'Kangchenjunga Climbed: An Account of the Climb by Both Men', in *Royal Geographical Society Journal*, vol. 122, March 1956

Guha, Ramachandra, *The Unquiet Woods: Ecological Change and Peasant Resistance in the Himalaya* (OUP India, 1989)

Jonas, Rudolf, *Im Garten der Göttlichen Nanda* (Austria, 1948)

Kapadia, Harish, 'Nanda Devi Juggernaut', in *Himalayan Journal*, vol. 58, 2002

King, Terry, 'Nanda North Face', in *Himalayan Journal*, vol. 36, 1978

Kohli, M.S. and Conboy, Kenneth, *Spies in the Himalayas* (The University Press of Kansas, 2002)

Kohn, Howard, 'The Nanda Devi Caper', in *Outside*, May 1978

Kumar, Narinder, *Nilakantha: The First Ascent* (New Delhi, 1963)

Kumar, Narinder, 'Nanda Devi: Indian Mountaineering Expedition 1964', in *Mountain World*, 1964–5

Languepin, J.-J., *Nanda Devi: 3e Expedition Francaise à L'Himalaya* (Arthaud, Paris, 1952)

Languepin, J.-J., *Himalaya, Passion Cruelle* (Flammarion, Paris, 1955), translated as *A Kiss to High Heaven* (William Kimber, 1956)

Leamer, Laurence, *Ascent: The Spiritual and Physical Quest of Willi Unsoeld* (New York, 1982)

Mason, Kenneth, *Abode of Snow* (London, 1955)

Mehta, Soli and Kapadia, Harish, *Exploring the Hidden Himalaya* (Hodder & Stoughton, 1990)

Mumm, A.L. *Five Months in the Himalayas* (London, 1907)

Murray, W.H., *The Evidence of Things Not Seen* (Baton Wicks, 2002)

Roper, Robert, *Fatal Mountaineer: The High Altitude Life and Death of Willi Unsoeld, American Himalayan Legend* (St Martin's Press, New York, 2002)

Roskelly, John, *Nanda Devi: The Tragic Expedition* (Stackpole, Harrisburg, 1987)

Sanan, Deepak, *Nanda Devi: Restoring Glory* (New Delhi, 1993)

Sax, William S., *Mountain Goddess: Gender and Politics in a Himalayan Pilgrimage* (OUP, 1993)

Sayle, Murray, 'The Vulgarity of Success', in *London Review of Books*, vol. 20, May 1998

Shipton, Eric, *Nanda Devi* (London, 1936), reprinted with an introduction by Charles Houston in Eric Shipton and H.W. Tilman, *Nanda Devi: Exploration and Ascent* (Baton Wicks, 1999)

Shipton, Eric, 'The Inviolate Sanctuary of the Blessed Goddess', in *Illustrated London News*, 12 January 1935

Shipton, Eric, 'Survey in the Nanda Devi District', in *Alpine Journal*, vol. 49, 1937, reprinted in Shipton and Tilman, *Nanda Devi: Exploration and Ascent* (Baton Wicks, 1999)

Shipton, Eric, *Upon That Mountain* (London, 1943)

Shipton, Eric, 'Some Reflections on Modern Climbing', in *Alpine Journal*, 1967

Shipton, Eric, *That Untravelled World* (London, 1969)

Shipton, Eric, *The Six Mountain Travel Books* (reissue: London, 1985)

Shipton, John, 'Nanda Devi Expedition 2000: Leader's Report' (private circulation)

Steele, Peter, *Eric Shipton – Everest and Beyond* (Constable, 1998)

Tilman, H.W., *The Ascent of Nanda Devi* (CUP, 1938), reprinted in Shipton and Tilman, *Nanda Devi: Exploration and Ascent* (Baton Wicks, 1999)

Vincent, Paul, *Nanda Devi: L'Ascension Impossible* (Paris, 1976)

Weber, T., *Hugging the Trees: The Story of the Chipko Movement* (Viking Penguin, New York, 1987)

Weir, Thomas, *The Ultimate Mountains* (London, 1953)

Young, A.J., 'A Flight in the Region of Nanda Devi, 1939', with notes by Eric Shipton, in *Royal Geographical Society Journal*, vol. 104, December 1944

INDEX